The Listener's Guide to Country Music

THE · LISTENER'S · GUIDE · TO
Country
Music

**Robert K. Oermann
with Douglas B. Green**

BLANDFORD PRESS

POOLE   DORSET

A Quarto Book

Copyright © 1983 by Quarto Marketing Ltd.

First published in the UK in 1983 by
Blandford Press
Link House, West Street
Poole, Dorset BH15 1LL

British Library Cataloguing in Publication Data
Oermann, Robert K.
The listener's guide to country music.
1. Country music—History and criticism.
I. Title   II. Green, Douglas B.
784.5′2′00973   ML3524

ISBN 0 7137 1351 8

The Listener's Guide to Country Music
was produced and prepared by
Quarto Marketing Ltd.
212 Fifth Avenue,
New York, New York 10010

Editor: **Gene Santoro**
Editorial Assistant: **Richard Selman**
Designer: **Abby Kagan**

Typesetting: BPE Graphics, Inc.
Printed and bound in the United States by
the Maple-Vail Group.

All photos courtesy of *THE COUNTRY MUSIC
FOUNDATION LIBRARY AND MEDIA CENTER.*
Special thanks to Kayce Cawthon.

CONTENTS

INTRODUCTION

Country music: you hear it, hear about it, daily. Its current popularity is a fact of life; you do not have to be a trained musicologist to hear the deep emotion, a sense of worth and of time, of value and of place, of a broad sweep of history, of folklore not as an antiquarian study but as a living thing. At its best country music is all this and more: it is music of the most direct and powerful expression of feelings, the voice of the people of America without regard to region, income, or education. This is its greatness.

The study of this greatness—and near-greatness—is what makes a joy of compiling this *Listener's Guide,* with the beginner and/or casual listener in mind. There are fine histories (*Country Music USA, The Illustrated History of Country Music,* and more) for those who wish to acquire more facts, a great many good biographies for those who want to investigate the lives of Bob Wills, Jimmie Rodgers, and others, and serious studies of types of songs ("Long Steel Rail," "Only A Miner," "He Was Singin' This Song"). For a comprehensive beginner's bibliography, see the Appendix. For us, the authors, there is the joy of sharing the music which has had enormous impact on our lives, the delight in compiling lists and making notes and comments on all the musical moments which have meant so much to us.

For it does not take a sophisticated musical ear to sense that there is much dross in country music. In fact, its propensity to be crass, obvious, smarmy, bathetic, trite, xenophobic, and overly cute has been a cross students and advocates of country music have had to bear over the years; it's hard to speak of greatness in a music filled with the heart and soul of a land when the tender, poetic strains of "Elvira" are rattling the speakers. So what we have done here is to sort and separate the precious material from the dross. It is an enjoyable process, for it reminds us, too, of the greatest moments in a recorded music's history.

A word of caution to the neophyte: Many of the singers and musicians, especially in the early period, perform music remote to modern sensibilities. Many took extensive liberties with time signatures, many played and sang badly out of tune; some sing with exaggerated emotion, while others sing with the curious emotionless affect that somehow emphasizes the power of the lyrics they recite. These things take getting used to, but it is well worth the effort, time, and trouble.

And it must be said, of course, that our choices are subjective; they could be no other. As you listen to these recordings and become familiar with them, some will strike you with intensity beyond all reason, and some will strike you as unappealing for any of a hundred reasons. Choose and grow with your likes, focus on a particular style—bluegrass or western swing or Cajun—or dote on the entire oeuvre of Jerry Lee Lewis or Bradley Kincaid or George Jones. Choose and explore the sounds and styles and performers who move you. This is how we all started, and when some strain of greatness appeals to you, and you become happily, intimately acquainted with it, you'll want to share it with your friends. This is, in just a slightly different way, exactly what we are doing in *The Listener's Guide To Country Music.*

A final discographical note before we begin: We have striven to cover only records which are or have recently been in print. Many of country music's great albums were discontinued long ago; many cuts have never been released on album. Reissues by the major labels are spotty, inconsistent, and infrequent. Many smaller labels have obtained reissue rights to older material, so even though you may have to search a bit to find reissues on Rounder, County, and other specialty labels, it is well worth your time and effort; in fact, it will be essential should you become a true devotee. Record numbers have been included to make your search easier. We can only hope as time goes by that interest in historical country music will bring about even more reissued classics.

Good luck. Have fun. We have!

Chapter One

A Historical Overview

There were no country music stars before the country music recording industry came to be. Before that time professionalism—with the notable exception of Uncle Dave Macon and the array of medicine show performers who are a part of the tradition—was virtually unknown. Country music was simply the plangent rhythm of the rocking chair and the wagon wheel, the square dance and the lumber camp, the quilting bee, the roundup, the harvest, the songs of courtship and of worship from rural America.

As we noted in the Introduction, several fine histories exist, and there is no need to recapitulate them here (see the Appendix for a bibliography); what we hope to impart is the feeling that is the essence of country music, not just the facts. Still, it is useful to know that this music evolved from the folksongs and fiddle tunes of the very first settlers to these shores.

Slavery then brought musicians from Africa, and the music of two cultures met and shared much. Successive immigration brought the Irish love of lyric and lilting melody; the lively dance, sense of beat, and the accordion from the Nordic and German settlers; the warm sound of the vaquero's guitar. Professional songwriters from what was becoming "Tin Pan Alley" ground out new songs, many of which trickled south and west to become a part of the folksinger's repertoire as well. The minstrel show brought a sense of show business and madcap fun; the Great Revival brought a host of powerful new religious songs.

The advent of recording caught all of that panorama and froze it for a moment in time, from the polished stentorian tenor of Vernon Dalhart to the raw vocalizing and minimalist playing of Henry Whitter; from the rough and rowdy Skillet Lickers' loose fiddle ensemble to the flowing architectural construction of Eck Robertson's Texas fiddle solos. These were country music's first releases, and the records of the 1920s were a vivid polyglot of all these elements and more: genuine folksongs, fiddle tunes old and new, cowboy laments and work tunes, plaintive modal banjo solos of harrowing loneliness.

It was inevitable that a sense of marketplace should begin to make itself felt in the country music of the late 1920s and early 1930s, for suddenly music had become a commercial venture. Though the genuine folk roots receded, the 1930s proved to be the most fertile, finest decade country music has ever had in terms of creativity, diversity, and energy—a genuine musical growth which has yet to be matched. The Depression era saw the rise of the singing cowboy on screen and record, of western swing, nascent honky-tonk, and several other completely diverse styles. Individual stars were being made, a profession was being shaped, and an astonishing variety of great music was created.

The war and postwar years saw less fertile musical development, but there was instead a continuing refinement of what already existed as well as an increasing emphasis on individual singing stars; however, some new forms, such as bluegrass, were created in this period. This trend toward a star system, toward thoroughly professional singers and songwriters, toward hit parades and agencies and the growth of Nashville as a major business and recording center continued unabated through the mid-1950s, when rockabilly shook the musical world for a time. It was greeted in some quarters with the same welcome that would be given the four horsemen of the Apocalypse —and with same reason. Rockabilly did sweep away much of what had come before, but in the long run it also laid the basis for the rise of "The Nashville Sound" as an antidote to its own raw vitality.

The most recent two decades of country music have proven to be its most dramatic in terms of measurable growth—records produced and charted and sold, concert grosses, television exposure, number of country radio stations, and the like. Yet they have been oddly static, too, as country music, in appealing to the largest numbers, has lost much of its original soul and energy. Stars have come and gone or come and stayed, substyles such as bluegrass have flourished outside the mainstream, musical power centers have shifted across the nation and back, but trends are much less defined while the music becomes more and

more homogeneous, filling the place of what was once
called "pop," for the listeners who find the remote
melodies of Ted Nugent or Blondie beyond their wish
to explore. Yet there have been many moments of glory
in recent country music as well, moments of elegant
simplicity and astonishing complexity, great vocals,
great records, great songs.

There is tremendous immediacy, enthusiasm, intense feeling, genuine emotion, pure spontaneity in
the country music of all eras. The following compilation albums cover the gamut, from earliest to latest.

Country music is simple music. Unlike jazz and
rock, it does not encompass highly disparate substyles; and it seldom features highly complex instrumentation, chord changes, or arrangements. Nonetheless, there are a number of historical and contemporary country genres that make this popular music
form more internally diverse than it appears to be.

Cajun, gospel, honky-tonk, western swing, bluegrass, rockabilly, old-time, singing cowboy, Nashville
Sound, country-rock, Anglo-American folk song,
country boogie, and dozens of smaller styles fall under
the country music umbrella. We'll deal with all of
these in these pages, but perhaps the best way a
novice can get an overview that compares and contrasts country's various forms is to acquire one of the
multidisc sets that brings the styles together in complete packages.

SELECTED RECORDINGS

The Smithsonian Collection of Classic Country Music
Smithsonian Institution (eight-record set)
This expensive boxed set covers a wide spectrum of
country music in 143 songs. It begins with Eck
Robertson's 1922 "Sallie Goodin' " and ends with
Willie Nelson's 1975 "Blue Eyes Crying In the Rain."
In between these, virtually every musical genre is
covered, although rockabilly is passed over and
bluegrass is given extra emphasis. Most of country's
most important and influential stars are covered as
well. An intelligently written 54-page booklet by
premier country historian Bill Malone makes this set
extra-valuable as a beginner's teaching aid. This is
both an excellent place to begin a country collection and an essential addition to any collection in
existence.

The Greatest Country Music Recordings of All Time
*The Franklin Mint Recording Society with The
Country Music Foundation*
This is a subscription set that is projected to reach
100 albums. Each month you receive a theme

double-LP set. In each attractively-bound box are two high-quality albums (24 songs, usually), a letter from the Society, and a well-illustrated essay booklet. Thus, in a set on bluegrass the subscriber gets music, visuals, and reading. Taken together, the packages' contents fully explain each country style. Of the overviews of country music available, this one seems most complete.

Country and Western Classics *Time-Life Records*

This is another subscription set. Fewer sets are planned than the Franklin Mint is offering, but those that have been issued cover their subjects in greater detail. In this series you get four discs per set and more scholarly booklets. Although the Time-Life series would arguably make better library material, its emphasis on detail rather than overview makes it less attractive for a beginner.

Chapter Two
Old-Time Music

Old-time country music is probably the least accessible to modern ears, yet many devotees find it the most moving, the most rewarding of all. It is country music as it was found in the 1920s by such early record company field recording men as Ralph Peer and Arthur Satherley, who found that a "market" existed for such homespun sounds, although the recording industry was then nearly 45 years old.

In fact, there proved to be a substantial audience for this music, which dates, on record, from Eck Robertson and Henry Gilliland's June 30 and July 1 sessions in 1922, and was quickly evidenced by Vernon Dalhart's 1925 multimillionseller "The Prisoner's Song/Wreck Of The Old 97." The music, from the very beginning, ran the gamut from raw, wild fiddle tunes to genteel ballads, from harsh (and sometimes nearly unintelligible) tales of the mill, mine, and prairie to polished instrumental trios and accomplished lyric soloists. Much of it was pure folk music, much of it was pure vaudeville; above all, it was sincere. There was little guile, coyness, or shameless playing to an audience—this was music played and sung as it was felt, and this is ultimately its joy and its greatness.

The world of commercial music quickly made itself felt: a more audience-oriented, sales-oriented sensibility soon pervaded country music, bringing new delights and problems, though old-time music existed and thrived well into the 1930s. Favorite performers like the Carter Family, for example, chose not to adapt their style to changing tastes of a faster-moving entertainment world, but played in their way to their audience till the end of their career.

Old-time country music is one of the most difficult genres to find on record except for the massive historical compilations touched on in the previous chapter; however, several smaller labels, County in particular among the most accessible, carry an extensive line of 1920s reissues. Although the traditional market for old time country music has dealt largely with the musicologist and historian, nonetheless a great deal of pleasure can be found here by the pure fan or neophyte; and indeed, much of this music is absolutely essential to an understanding of what followed.

THE CARTER FAMILY

Born in the isolated foothills of the Clinch Mountains of Virginia, Alvin Pleasant Carter (1891-1960), his wife Sara Dougherty Carter (1899-1979), and his brother Ezra's wife Maybelle Addington Carter (1909-1978) comprised one of country music's cornerstone groups.

A.P.—sometimes known as Doc—led The Carter Family, arranged and collected the music, and sang bass. Sara sang lead and took the majority of the vocal solos in a deep, rich, haunting voice. She also played guitar and autoharp. Maybelle sang harmony, played steel guitar occasionally, and popularized the autoharp as a melody instrument. This was in addition to her developing a revolutionary and extremely influential guitar style, in which she played melody on the bass strings and brushed the treble strings for rhythm. This technique was widely imitated in guitar history.

The trio first recorded for Ralph Peer in Bristol, Tennessee, on August 1, 1927, the same week as Jimmie Rodgers. It was here that A.P.'s song collecting was discovered. Peer's Southern Music began publishing the magnificent collection of folk and parlor songs Carter had been gathering for years, and would continue to gather throughout his life.

The Carter Family's early impact on record was great, with "Bury Me Under the Weeping Willow" (1928), "Thinking Tonight of My Blue Eyes" (1929), "My Clinch Mountain Home" (1929), "Foggy Mountain Top" (1929), "Lulu Wall" (1930), "Sweet Fern" (1930), "Lonesome Valley" (1931), "You Are My Flower" (1937), "Jealous Hearted Me" (1937), and of course the country guitarists' standard "Wildwood Flower" (1928) being outstanding releases. They did very little touring, however. In fact, in 1929 when their record sales were at a peak, A.P. and Sara were living in working-class Detroit while Maybelle and Ezra were in similar circumstances in Washington, D.C.! Despite their inability to cash in on their disc success, they continued to record extensively for years for Victor (1927-1934), ARC (1935-1936), Decca (1936-1938), Columbia/ Okeh (1940), and for Victor once again (1940).

From 1938 to 1941 they made their only real attempt at making a living as professional musicians, playing at the Mexican border stations XEG, XENT, and XERA near Del Rio, Texas. But A.P. and Sara's divorce, Sara's remarriage, and changing public tastes finally caused the breakup of the group in 1943.

Sara and her new husband Coy Bayes immediately moved to California; A.P. returned to the Clinch Mountains to record only sporadically with his children Joe and Janette, while Maybelle continued a successful musical career with her daughters Helen, June, and Anita.

With this group—adding and subtracting daughters and other musicians as the need arose (Chet Atkins, Jan Howard, and Bobbie Harden among them)— Maybelle continued to perform, until her death, with son-in-law Johnny Cash. Her popularity kept the Carter fame and heritage alive into the modern country music era.

The Carter Family's contributions extend far beyond their record sales alone. Their remarkable repertoire of old-timey and folk song material; their influential group harmony sound and its stark, haunting quality; and the instrumental genius of Maybelle Carter, unquestionably one of the handful of most influential musicians in the entire history of country music, make them the most important group in old-time music.

THE SKILLET LICKERS

An extremely popular and influential Atlanta-based string band of the 1920s and 1930s pioneered the southeastern old-time style. The Skillet Lickers, led by Gid Tanner, included two other country music figures of towering importance in their own right: fiddler Clayton McMichen and singer/guitarist Riley Puckett.

Tanner (1885-1960) first recorded with Puckett (1894-1946), a blind guitarist, for Columbia in 1924. He continued to record with various permutations of Skillet Lickers for Columbia and Victor for the next decade. The Georgia band did not formally take its name until 1926, when McMichen (1900-1970) joined Tanner, Puckett, and banjo player Fate Norris.

Skillet Licker material, for the most part, was composed of fiddle breakdowns, minstrel songs, and a bizarre and hilarious series of eighteen spoken comedy skits called "A Corn Licker Still In Georgia." The fiddle tune "Down Yonder" is probably most closely associated with the band.

The musicians' sound together was rough and wild, typically featuring the twin fiddling of McMichen and Bert Layne (a later member), falsetto shouts and snatches of verses from Tanner, and Puckett's bluesy singing. All three Skillet Licker mainstays went their separate ways after 1934, but the legacy of The Skillet Lickers is one of humorous, extremely good-natured old-time music played in the most spirited of styles. The Skillet Lickers were unique, but their sound was a form of old-time country music that was passing away even as they were recording it.

UNCLE DAVE MACON

Whereas the Carters and the Skillet Lickers represent the rustic rural roots of country music, Uncle Dave Macon was the quintessential reminder that even in its earliest commercial form, country music was show business. With their folk song repertoire the Carters sang of sad simplicity. With their fiddle tunes and breakdowns the Skillet Lickers commercialized the old-time dance music heritage. Uncle Dave was as country as both of those acts, but he was an outrageous ham who had the shrewd intuition that entertainment was more than just music.

He bridged the gap between 19th century show business and the beginnings of 20th century country music. His style incorporated vaudeville, minstrel show, medicine show, and gospel meeting elements so effectively that he easily made the transition to radio, records, and film. Although he did not embark on a professional country career until the age of 50, his years as a country entertainer were long and fruitful. By the time he died, he was one of the most beloved personalities in the field.

David Harrison Macon was born in Smart Station, Tennessee, on October 7, 1870. When he was 13 years old his father moved the family to nearby Nashville, where he bought the Broadway Hotel. Here young David soon fell under the spell of the vaudeville and circus entertainers who frequented the establishment, and learned to play the banjo from a popular musician and comedian named Joel Davidson.

After his father's death in 1888 the family moved to Readyville, and the following year Dave bought a nearby farm where he was to live right up until his death. Although he continued to play the banjo and entertain his friends and family, he spent the majority of his time working his farm, operating the Macon

Midway Mule and Wagon Transportation Company, and raising six sons.

He was first paid for performing his music in 1918, was playing regularly by 1921, and by 1923 he was in such demand that he began doing extensive tours for Loew's vaudeville circuit. In July of 1924 he made his first recordings, and by December of 1925 had joined the WSM Barn Dance—soon to be known as the Grand Ole Opry—an association that was to last twenty-six years. Uncle Dave continued to spend the bulk of his time on personal appearances and recordings, cutting over twenty sides a year between 1925 and 1930, despite his advancing age.

In the 1930s he became a fixture of the Opry, and recorded for Brunswick, Gennett, and Bluebird, even as late as 1938. In 1940 he appeared in a Republic film called *Grand Ole Opry,* giving an exuberant perform-ance (at the age of 70) of "Take Me Back To My Old Carolina Home."

Age, in fact, did not appreciably slow him down until 1950, when he finally gave up touring, although he continued appearing on the Grand Ole Opry up until March 1, 1952. He entered the Murfreesboro hospital the next day and died there three weeks later.

JIMMIE RODGERS

Although he wasn't country music's first recorded singer or even its first recording star, Jimmie Rodgers has probably had a more profound impact on country music than any other singer/songwriter in history. Not only did he influence the generation which followed him—Gene Autry, Jimmie Davis, Ernest Tubb, Hank Snow, and the like—but they in turn introduced still another generation to the sound and the charm of the Jimmie Rodgers style.

James Charles Rodgers was born in 1897, probably in Mississippi, the son of a railroad worker. Always interested in music, he was well enough known for his singing and banjo playing as an amateur while a young man. He evidently absorbed a great deal of musical style and culture from black railroad workers when he attempted to follow in his father's footsteps.

Although it is often assumed that Jimmie turned to music only after his advancing tuberculosis made hard physical labor on the railroad impossible, he had actually made several early stabs at a musical career. One attempt was in 1917; and in 1923 he toured with vaudevillian Billy Terrell's Comedians as a singer. It was not until 1924 that his tuberculosis was diagnosed. From that point on he worked less and less on the railroad, alternating that with musical work and stays in hospitals.

He wandered all over the country, including the far west, before settling in Asheville, North Carolina for a time and gaining his first radio show. There he got together with local musicians and formed the Jimmie Rodgers Entertainers. This group travelled to Bristol, Virginia to audition for Ralph Peer of Victor Records in early August, 1927. At the last minute, the group broke up and Jimmie recorded two numbers on his own, "Sleep Baby Sleep" and "The Soldier's Sweetheart."

While the records didn't set the world on fire, they did justify another recording session, this time at Victor headquarters in Camden, New Jersey. This was where he recorded the first of his famed Blue Yodels, "Blue Yodel #1 (T for Texas)." This marked the beginning of a long series of such recorded performances. The record was a huge success, selling a million copies, and within a year Jimmie Rodgers was a star.

His stay as one of America's most popular singers was short and difficult, for his health allowed only sporadic touring, and even as early as 1929 he was often too ill to appear. That same year, however, he did star in a musical film short, *The Singing Brakeman*. Viewed today, Jimmie's film image looks thin and tired, but his music sounds superb. He made records as often as possible—recording 111 sides in all—but he grew progressively weaker. A move to Texas, first to Kerrville, then to San Antonio, gave him a dry climate for his health, but little chance to rest because of his desire to provide well for his family with his music. He kept on travelling and recording.

While in New York, recording his final 24 numbers, Rodgers lapsed into a coma and died on May 26, 1933 at the age of 35. The entire South mourned.

Jimmie Rodgers's music is a fascinating mixture of country, blues, and sentimental pop tunes; and he recorded with a wide variety of backup bands and sounds. Nevertheless, he is often regarded as the Father of Country Music, and his influence cannot be overstated.

VERNON DALHART

Country music's very first million-selling record was sung by a man whose background was as a light opera tenor. It is ironic that the record that launched commercial country music wasn't even by a hillbilly.

Vernon Dalhart was a Texan, however. Born Marion Try Slaughter in 1883 in Jefferson, Texas, the singer was the son of a rancher. The Slaughters moved to

Dallas when he was a teenager, and there the young-ster attended the Dallas Conservatory of Music and began his career as a music salesman. Selling pianos, sheet music, and record players took him around the country. In time, he hit New York and successfully auditioned for Broadway musicals and light operas. Another main source of income was his onstage dem-onstrations of Edison phonographs. He would sing on stage, then play the Edison recording of him singing the same song to show how lifelike phonograph sound was. The Edison recordings, his first, began appearing in 1915.

It was not until he began recording country music, however, that Vernon Dalhart's recording career really took off. He had adopted the name Vernon Dalhart for his record performances by taking the names of two Texas towns ("Vernon" and "Dalhart") of his boyhood; and in 1924 he started recording tunes that recalled his young Texas years as well. Chief among these were "The Prisoner's Song" and "The Wreck of the Old '97," which the singer recorded for Victor Records that year. Both were his reworkings of earlier songs that had become part of the American folk tradition. Dalhart's heartfelt, yearning singing of both made them much more. They became commercial smash successes.

Thanks to Dalhart's recording of these numbers, commercial country music was launched in a big way, for his Victor record pairing the two songs sold well over a million copies. And that's not all: back in the 1920s there were not as many exclusive recording clauses. Thus, Vernon Dalhart also recorded "The Prisoner's Song" and "The Wreck of the Old '97" for several other companies. Eventually, the two songs appeared on over 50 different record labels; and al-most each one had a different artist's name on it. Dalhart, it seems, had well over 50 pseudonyms as a recording artist. It is said that he sometimes had three recording sessions a day to keep up with the demand for his voice. "Death of Floyd Collins," "My Blue Ridge Mountain Home," "Little Rosewood Casket," and sev-eral other numbers were huge hits for the prolific singer. Dalhart's lifetime record sales may be as high as 75 million!

Sadly, this one-man recording industry dropped completely out of sight during the Depression. As incredible as it sounds, his thousands of recordings were almost all made before 1929. Except for a final recording session in 1938, Vernon Dalhart's fabulously successful career was over by the close of the 1920s.

Fame went to poor Vernon's head. Reports from those who knew him well indicate that he was a difficult, arrogant man given to bursts of temper and prima donna behavior. When it came time for fame to fade, Dalhart had his pride and his beautiful voice, but not much else.

By the 1940s his money was all gone, his name was forgotten, and his vocal pupils were few. With his business cards advertising himself as a voice coach and his memories of more glorious days, he died in Bridgeport, Connecticut of a heart attack on September 14, 1948.

Dalhart's music combines the artful emotionalism of Irish tenors like John McCormick with the simple beauty of country melodies. He sang in a direct, clear style that is still attractive to modern ears. Because his was a trained, sophisticated voice he was able to sell hillbilly tunes to urban audiences. Because he was recorded with simple guitar/harmonica accompaniment his sound was equally attractive to Southern country folk.

CHARLIE POOLE

Charlie Poole was an adventurous banjoist, a charismatic performer, and a transitional figure in country music, for he fused the old-time banjo style of his Carolina mountains with his strong, peculiar vocals, a harbinger of the popular vocalists who would appear in the following decade.

Born in Alamance County, North Carolina, in 1892, he spent much of his life as a millworker and occasional entertainer, first recording (with fiddler Posey Rorer and guitarist Norman Woodleiff) for Columbia in July of 1925. The success of Charlie Poole and the North Carolina Ramblers was all too brief, for Poole's personal instability and the Depression made his live performances and recording dates haphazard things, though marked with flashes of musical greatness.

Poole died on May 21, 1931, of an apparent heart attack, but he left a legacy of rough and rowdy Carolina string band music and extremely advanced banjo playing important to this day, not so much for his musicianship, but for the songs he popularized, including "Don't Let Your Deal Go Down," "New Frankie and Johnnie," and "All Go Hungry Hash House."

BRADLEY KINCAID

Bradley Kincaid, one of country music's most influential performers of any era, was born in the foothills of the Cumberland Mountains on July 13, 1895. A singer from his youth, he put himself through college by singing many of the folk ballads of his youth on WLS in

Chicago, and he quickly became extremely popular on radio and on record.

His pure tenor was an ideal vehicle for the mountain folk songs in which he specialized—though he did perform love songs, cowboy songs, and others as well—and he was a popular radio star for two decades, often in the north and east, though he did spend five years on the Grand Ole Opry in the 1940s.

During the peak of his popularity he became the first country entertainer to publish a songbook—the bushel baskets full of orders delivered to WLS upon its release made it the harbinger of many songbooks to come. He continued to mine the Kentucky hills for old songs, and in a very real sense was a modern-day folk song collector, preserving (as did A.P. Carter) a wealth of traditional music while maintaining a successful commercial career.

In fact, Kincaid's career continued to be a success long after more commercial forms had replaced Kentucky folk ballads in popularity, a tribute to his magnetism as a performer. He eventually retired in the early 1950s to open a music store in Ohio, where he still lives in genial retirement, pushing 90.

CARSON J. ROBISON

Carson Robison's importance lies in the fact that he was one of the first country musicians to take a folk-based style and professionalize it. He composed, commercialized, and capitalized on country music's basic elements, creating one of the earliest catalogs of compositions specifically tailored to the country music ethos. Indeed, many of his better-known tunes are frequently mistaken for folk songs. His nasal, yet attractive, presentation of them has a tongue-in-cheek quality that shows he understood how to exploit a down-home personality as well as the Dolly Partons and Loretta Lynns of today.

Robison's formula of vaudeville, event songs, and hillbilly ditties made him one of the most popular country songwriters of his era. His abilities as an instrumentalist made him an active country-guitar accompanist in the recording studios as well. "Barnacle Bill the Sailor," "Carry Me Back To the Lone Prairie," "Little Green Valley," "Left My Gal In the Mountains," "Life Gets Tee-Jus, Don't It," and "My Blue Ridge Mountain Home" made him one of the outstanding country music pioneers. Born in Oswego, Kansas, in 1890, he moved to Kansas City in 1920, where he became one of the first country singers to be heard on the radio. He moved to New York in the early 1920s, where he recorded as early as 1924 with Vernon Dalhart (as guitarist, vocalist, and whistler), and indeed went into business with Dalhart, an association that lasted four years. He followed this association with a new partner, long-time New York country music singer and producer Frank Luther, before striking out on his own again, heading such outfits as the Pioneers, the Buckaroos, the Carson Robison Trio, and the Pleasant Valley Boys throughout the years. He remained active, performing and recording up until the time of his death in 1957.

Robison's work has tended to be overlooked, or at least has not had the lasting popularity of many of the string bands, or the Carter Family or Jimmie Rodgers. Still, his work was of great influence in its day, especially since he was one of the earliest of the true professionals in country music.

SELECTED RECORDINGS
ANTHOLOGIES:
Anthology of American Folk Music, Vols. 1-3
Folkways Records 2951-2953
This set is most significant for the wide range of old-time styles it covers. Dance tunes, folk songs, blues, ballads, and comic songs are all represented, as are most of the major personalities in old-time country music. Uncle Dave Macon, The Carter Family, Kelly Harrell, Charlie Poole, Dock Boggs, The Stonemans, Buell Kazee, Bascom Lamar Lunsford, and Frank Hutchison are just a few of the stylists represented in this large collection.

In addition, *The Anthology of American Folk Music* was the pioneering old-time music record reissue. Compiled in the 1950s, it virtually introduced the modern world to the pleasures of simple, rustic music from old 78s.

Smokey Mountain Ballads *RCA Camden ACL 1-7022*
This, too, is an excellent introduction to old-time music. There are several performances here in particular which are outstanding. The Monroe Brothers' eerie "What Does the Deep Sea Say," Arthur Smith's mock-tragic "Chittlin' Cookin' Time In Cheatham County," and The Carter Family's classic "Worried Man Blues" are special pleasures.

Victor Records was arguably the most important label in the recording of early country music, so the vaults of its descendant, RCA Records, are a treasure trove of old-time material. *Smokey Mountain Ballads* collects together examples of some of Victor's best vintage country acts.

Mountain Blues *County Records 511*

This album illustrates the cross-pollination that occurred between black and white rural musicians in
the early 20th-century South. As the record demonstrates, from the very beginnings of its commercial
existence country music had a strong blues strain.
Even today, there are people who describe country
music as white man's blues. Such hillbilly pioneers
as Frank Hutchison, Jimmie Tarlton, Sam McGee,
and The Leake County Revelers provide superb
support for this thesis with their performances on
this compilation.

Old Time Fiddle Classics *County Records 507*

Early country music was dominated by the fiddle.
Long before the rise of the guitar as a lead instrument, and many years before singing stars characterized country performances, fiddlers were sawing
away at jigs, reels, hornpipes, and breakdowns
(generally speaking, the four types of country fiddle
melodies). The first 78s reflected this.

This reissue spotlights country's venerable fiddle
tradition. Most of the major early fiddlers are represented, including such highly influential stylists as
Eck Robertson (the man who made America's first
authentic country disc), Clayton McMichen (perhaps the most important and imitated old-time fiddler), and Arthur Smith (often considered the best
of the lot).

Steel Guitar Classics *Old Timey Records 113*

The steel guitar actually didn't assume that great a
role in country music until well after the old-time
music era; but this LP demonstrates that its distinctive sound colored country discs even in the early
years. Hawaiian bands had introduced country
pickers to the steel sound. Thus, this disc presents
the work of Sol Hoopi's Trio and Kanui & Lula as
well as country steel guitar pioneers such as Jimmie
Tarlton, Cliff Carlisle, and Jenks "Tex" Carmen.
The bands of Roy Acuff and Jimmie Davis are also
showcased. The resulting compilation is a listening
joy from start to finish.

Songs of the Railroad *Vetco Records 103*

Unlike many old-time music reissue albums, this
one focuses on a theme. Years ago, the railroad had
a tremendous mystique in America, especially to
rural dwellers. Train songs, therefore, have always
occupied a place of pride in country musicians'
repertoires.

But besides being an interesting collection of
songs, this LP is a fine introduction to several significant country music pioneers. Fiddlin' John Carson,

often cited as hillbilly music's first rural "star," is represented, as is country's first million-selling artist, Vernon Dalhart. Henry Whitter, another of the first hillbillies to make records, is featured, too. Al Hopkins, one of The Grand Ole Opry's earliest performers, and The Pickard Family, an extremely important popularizer of American folk music on radio, are also included on this large, fine, 16-song compilation.

Nashville: The Early String Bands
County Records 541, 542 (two-record set)
The first recording session ever held in Music City was in the fall of 1928. Victor Records recorded the rustic string bands of the infant Grand Ole Opry (begun in 1925) on that occasion. First to record were The Binkley Brothers Clodhoppers; and among the others to step up to the record company's microphone were the Opry's first performer, Uncle Jimmy Thompson; Nashville's first radio string band, Dr. Humphrey Bate's Possum Hunters; and the Opry's black harmonica wizard, Deford Bailey.

These two records preserve that historically significant event. They also provide an excellent window onto the world of middle-Tennessee traditional music of that faraway time.

Although there were certainly many gifted fiddlers, guitarists, and banjo players in Nashville at the time, one striking feature of the Opry's early string bands was that many featured the harmonica as a lead instrument. Thus, some of the music captured by Victor's 1928 microphones consisted of the fiddle tune heritage transposed for harmonica solos. This fact makes many of the early Nashville string band 78s unique, and makes this record an outstanding document.

INDIVIDUAL PERFORMERS:
● The Carter Family
Mid the Green Fields of Virginia
RCA Records ANL-1107
Since The Carter Family's role as a preserver and popularizer of folk songs, 19th-century parlor songs, and musical Americana is unmatched by any other act, a compilation of their work is essential to any country music record collection. It contains many of their homespun masterpieces, such as "Keep On the Sunny Side" (their theme song), "Foggy Mountain Top," "Picture On the Wall," "Will You Miss Me When I'm Gone?," "Bury Me Under the Weeping Willow," and "My Clinch Mountain Home."

The uninitiated often complain that all Carter performances sound alike. But relaxing alone and allowing them to weave their warm, intimate, living-room spell allows the three's nuances to be heard. Once you've come to know The Carter Family, this is an album from which to draw strength, solace, peace, and pleasure.

● **The Skillet Lickers**
Old Time Tunes Recorded 1927-1931
County Records 506
The Skillet Lickers is perhaps not the best act to acquire as an introduction to old-time music. Their chaotic, raucous, full-tilt style is off-putting to most nonmusicians. Fiddlers, on the other hand, find tremendous delight in the band's crazy expertise.

This reissue emphasizes those instrumental qualities. Although The Skillet Lickers performed notable renditions of ballads, pop tunes, and vaudeville-derived novelties, this disc offers a cross-secton of the band's traditional dance melodies and fiddle pieces. The album offers ample proof of why Clayton McMichen (and, to a lesser extent, Gid Tanner) stood at the forefront of hoedown fiddlers.

● **Riley Puckett**
Waitin' For the Evening Mail *County Records 411*
McMichen's opinion was that it was Riley Puckett's singing that sold The Skillet Lickers' records. The blind Puckett was also one of his era's finest guitarists, capable of dazzling double-time runs and dextrous picking. *Waitin' For the Evening Mail* is dedicated to the proposition that McMichen's praise was well-placed. In his day, Riley Puckett was regarded as highly among country musicians as Jimmie Rodgers; but for many years his recordings remained unavailable and his reputation slipped. This reissue should help to restore his stature, for Puckett remains an engaging singer, even to modern ears; and his tune choices were always excellent.

● **Uncle Dave Macon**
Early Recordings *County Records 521*
A natural born showman with wonderfully rollicking, charming, eccentric qualities like Uncle Dave's probably has to be seen to be fully appreciated. His records probably only hint at what a delight he must have been to watch.

Regardless of their value as documents of his live-performance abilities, however, Uncle Dave Macon's 78s remain joyous listening experiences. This County reissue of some of them includes well-known Macon favorites like "Sail Away Ladies," "Rabbit In the Pea Patch," and "Rock About My Sarah Jane" that demonstrate the old man's tremendous energy and verve, as well as numbers like "Just One Way to the Pearly Gates" that demonstrate his unique singing abilities.

There is no such thing as a bad Uncle Dave Macon reissue LP. No lover of American humor can fail to be charmed by his records. No lover of banjo styles would want to be without some. And even if today's reissue albums reveal only a fraction of his gifts, they stand on their own as entertainment.

Macon was really a rather ordinary banjo stylist of the frailing, or drop-thumb style. Like the modern-day Grandpa Jones he tended to beat away at the instrument rather than drawing subtleties from it. He also tended to shout his lyrics, rather than sing them, and he could be quite cavalier about melodies and lyrics. This, and nearly every other Dave Macon record, reminds us that the whole is sometimes greater than the sum of its parts; for, all in all, the man remains one of the most striking and memorable country musicians who ever lived.

● Jimmie Rodgers
This Is Jimmie Rodgers
RCA Records VPS-6091 (two-record set)
Alone among old-time musicians, America's Blue Yodeller strikes an instantly familiar musical chord even now, for echoes of his voice can still be heard in the performers of today. His style and songs transcend the barrier of time almost completely, because his engaging personality was in every note he sang. His brilliant blend of musical elements from the blues, ragtime, hillbilly, vaudeville, and pop song traditions continues to delight new fans year after year. Indeed, Jimmie Rodgers records are almost everyone's introduction to old-time country music. If Maybelle Carter is country's pioneer instrumentalist, then Jimmie Rodgers is its pioneer vocalist and songwriter.

Rodgers left us classic tunes like "Waiting For a Train," "T for Texas," "Muleskinner Blues," and lilting, jazzy melodies in profusion. The best of them are collected in this fine two-record introduction to his music. It is ample proof that Rodgers will never stop singing; The Singing Brakeman is immortal.

● Vernon Dalhart
Ballads and Railroad Songs
Old Homestead Records OHCS-129
Listening to this compilation of his work, you can easily understand Vernon Dalhart's phenomenal popularity. He was an extremely pleasant singer,

full of sincerity, natural tone, and relaxation. Carson Robison's tasteful guitar playing was the perfect foil for Dalhart's Texas drawl on many of their recorded performances. The songs themselves are often timely jewels of the period's sentiments and opinions; witness Dalhart's readings of the likes of "In the Baggage Coach Ahead," "Putting On the Style," "The Sinking of the Titanic," "In the Hills of Old Kentucky," "Casey Jones," and "Little Mary Phagan," all included here. In addition to being so historically significant, as music this survives the test of time very well indeed.

He is rather stiff and formal as country singers go, but Vernon Dalhart can still be most enjoyable. Unfortunately, he has not been well-served by reissue albums, and this, with its rather poor sound quality, is the only easily obtainable Dalhart disc still around.

● Charlie Poole
Charlie Poole and the North Carolina Ramblers
County Records 505, 509 (two-record set)
Poole was a crazed, brilliant country genius who drank himself into an early grave at age 29. Fortunately, he left behind a legacy of songs that includes such gems as "Don't Let Your Deal Go Down," "If the River Was Whiskey," "Take a Drink On Me," "White House Blues," and "It's Movin' Day." Also fortunately, the two albums of his work on County Records have reissued these and many other Poole performances. These records fully explain this old-time musician's greatness. He was part bluesman, part jokester, part picker, and part sentimental balladeer. Along with The Blue Sky Boys and the Mainers, Charlie Poole is North Carolina's superior gift to old-time country music. Almost his entire recorded repertoire and disc output was in the distant 1920s, but his performances remain fresh and fascinating. The lazy, jazzy, bluesy qualities he possesses are timeless indeed.

● Bradley Kincaid
Bradley Kincaid *Old Homestead Records*
Kincaid's high, precise tenor is not everyone's cup of tea. He has a certain warmth, but none of Dalhart's downhome, natural quality. His presentation tends to be somewhat flat and dull; and his songs are sometimes too long and too familiar. Still, he is one of the most widely popular country stars who ever lived. And invariably, those who remember old-time radio remember Bradley Kincaid with great affection. This is the only available reissue of his work.

● Carson Robison
The Immortal Carson Robison
Glendale Records GL-6009
● Carson Robison
Just a Melody *Old Homestead Records OHCS-134*

After Carson Robison broke away from Vernon
Dalhart he turned toward cowboy imagery and continued as one of country music's major songwriters.
He became a nationally broadcast NBC radio star in
the 1930s, the time of the performances on the
Glendale reissue LP. Of all the reissues in this
section, this one comes closest to capturing the
ambiance of Depression-era radio. It brings you
virtually a complete old-time broadcast.

Just a Melody, on the other hand, contains a more
complete cross-secton of his repertoire. Two of his
most famous compositions, "My Blue Ridge Mountain Home" and "Barnacle Bill the Sailor," are included, as well as Robison's version of contemporary country songwriting pioneer Bob Miller's
"Eleven Cent Cotton and Forty Cent Meat." The
man had taste and talent; either disc demonstrates
that much.

Chapter Three
__Bluegrass__

Bluegrass music somehow suggests a wilder yet simpler time, with the fire and drive of the five-string banjo, the bluesy wail of the fiddle, the eerie, moving, intense singing often called the "high lonesome sound." It is the archaic, stubborn, proud music of a people and of a region; and it is in large part a music shaped by Bill Monroe, who galvanized the mid-1940s sound.

A direct outgrowth of the old-time stringband, bluegrass added the intensity and power of Monroe's mandolin playing and his powerful singing and songwriting, an updated fiddle style, and the new and exciting banjo style of 20 year old Earl Scruggs in 1945. By 1950 several bands around the country were adopting this driving acoustic style, innovative yet rich with tradition.

Bluegrass saw hard times in the late 1950s, but it was discovered during the folk revival period of the early 1960s, and began a remarkable growth undreamed of until then. By the end of the decade banjos and fiddles were heard on film and TV soundtracks, commercials, and in hundreds of festivals crowding the summer months; indeed, the term bluegrass—which we define here a bit more rigidly—has for many people come to mean any acoustic-oriented music which seems to convey a mystical sense of rural paradise, of certain solid, unchanging values in a swiftmoving and increasingly urban society.

Perhaps most interesting of all, bluegrass continues to grow and thrive outside of the commercial mainstream. Rarely heard on radio (except, occasionally, on programs devoted strictly to bluegrass), it has found its own homegrown method of marketing: the social event known as the bluegrass festival, and the small record label. It is music of intensity, and bluegrass fans as a whole may be the most passionate, intense fans in country music.

BILL MONROE

There have been but a handful of true stylistic inventors in country music, and Bill Monroe is without question prominent among them. His was the force and vision which created bluegrass as a style, which sustained it through the good years and lean, and which continues to sustain it spiritually, though it has in the past decade branched into directions he might never have dreamed of.

Bill was born September 13, 1911 in Rosine, Kentucky, on the western edge of the state's bluegrass region, hence the name of his band and ultimately the entire musical genre. He learned a rich musical tradition from his mother, his elder brothers, from a fiddler uncle he celebrated in song ("Uncle Pen"), and from a black guitarist, fiddler, and railroad worker named Arnold Schultz, who gave to Monroe's music the powerful touch of blues which is one of its most distinct elements.

Bill and his elder brother Charlie, a strong guitarist and singer and a forceful stage personality, formally teamed up in 1935 as the Monroe Brothers, and in the three short years of their professional partnership they electrified audiences across the southeast, adding a drive and excitement theretofore unknown in duet singing.

Each brother formed his own band in 1938, and in 1939 Bill and his Blue Grass Boys won a job on the Grand Ole Opry. His debut performance at that venerable institution presaged what was to come: numerous ovations for an old blues number "Mule Skinner Blues," which combined all the elements which exemplify bluegrass, save one. It was high pitched, with a crackling yodel; the fiddle was mournful, bluesy, yet somehow driven; the guitar pulsed with a syncopated rhythm.

The missing element was the banjo. Always willing to allow talented musicians to propel his music in new directions, Monroe added a shy kid from North Carolina named Earl Scruggs in 1945 who solidified the sound and style of bluegrass music. The music of this 1945–1948 version of the Blue Grass Boys (in addition to Monroe and Scruggs, were Lester Flatt on guitar and "Chubby" Wise on fiddle) has ever since been the standard against which all others have been compared since.

As popular as they may be, all styles experience advances and declines, and by the late 1950s few but Monroe's most loyal fans stuck by him. Fewer and fewer good musicians came his way, and those that did didn't stay long: too much time between jobs. Yet right at this dark time another whole wave of interest was growing, for the folk music movement beginning to catch on with America's collegiates embraced bluegrass with enthusiasm. Within a few short years the entire field went from what looked like an exquisite but dying art form to a music of enormous popularity.

Through it all the regal, proud figure of Bill Monroe reigned. Proclaimed the "father of bluegrass" early on, he continues to this day to perform with his Blue Grass Boys, his powerful tenor voice and highly charged mandolin playing having changed the course of country music, giving it one of its most exciting and yet tradition-oriented of all its substyles.

LESTER FLATT AND EARL SCRUGGS

In their 21 years as a team, Flatt and Scruggs doubtless introduced more people to bluegrass music than any other outfit. The first bluegrass act to achieve true national prominence, they were one of the most popular and influential teams in country music history.

They met in 1945, when Bill Monroe hired Scruggs—who was born near Shelby, North Carolina, in 1924; Flatt, a superb singer, fine songwriter, and influential rhythm guitarist had at that time been with the Blue Grass Boys for about a year. They left within a few months of each other in 1948, and in the space of a few months had formed their own group, the Foggy Mountain Boys.

Their recording career began almost immediately, for Mercury and then for Columbia, and by 1955 they were members of the Grand Ole Opry, where their sponsorship by Martha White Mills helped see them through the rock and roll years. Their early cuts are some of the finest bluegrass music ever recorded: confident, compelling, showcasing Scruggs's dynamic banjo playing (still unequalled in feel and excitement) as well as Flatt's fine songwriting and easygoing lead voice. A host of superb bandmembers—most notably awesome fiddler Benny Martin—have joined them through the years. Although some hit records came their way in the 1960s ("The Ballad of Jed Clampett," "Foggy Mountain Breakdown" from the film *Bonnie and Clyde*) their music had begun to lose its freshness, mellowing at times into listlessness.

This, and their ever-diverging musical interests finally caused their split in 1969. Flatt put together a

Flatt and Scruggs were the first bluegrass act to
achieve true national prominence.

basically old-time bluegrass ensemble with all acoustic instruments, and continued to perform with his
Nashville Grass up until his death in 1979 at the age of
65. Scruggs, ten years his junior, formed the Earl
Scruggs Revue with his talented sons, and continues a
successful performing and recording career.

Bill Monroe has worn the mantle of Father of Bluegrass Music with justification, for it was his vision, his
style, his dominating presence that forged the band
that named the music. Still, without the rapid, three-
fingered, revolutionary banjo picking of Earl Scruggs,
bluegrass music would never have acquired its special
sound. Scruggs's contribution was easily as important
as Bill's intense tenor singing and deft mandolin playing in defining bluegrass.

THE STANLEY BROTHERS

Though very young at the time, the Stanley Brothers of
McClure, Virginia were among the very first emulators
of Bill Monroe's style (not yet called bluegrass) when
they signed with Columbia Records in 1949—Carter
was but 24, Ralph just 22. Their style was quite distinctive, being softer, more eerie, more primitive in feel,
though not lacking in musicianship.

Carter, the guitarist, wrote a great many bluegrass
songs—possibly too many, as their quality varied in
extremes—but at his best captured with precision the
essence of lonesome mountain soul. And his haunting
lead vocals, paired with Ralph's clenched tenor, were
beautiful and unforgettable.

Ralph, a traditional banjo player adept at both bluegrass and old-time styles, kept the Stanley sound alive

after Carter's early death in 1966, and has been involved in an astonishing number of recordings. Much of the early Stanley Brothers' material has been reissued by Rounder, while Rebel Records has recorded a bushel basket full of Ralph Stanley albums featuring various versions of his everchanging band.

It is beautiful, haunting, soulful mountain music at its best, and not to be missed.

DON RENO AND RED SMILEY

Reno and Smiley were one of the first of the early bluegrass groups to establish a distinct and unique vision for the sound. Their chief distinction was Don Reno's banjo style. He developed it quickly from the traditional style (he was one of a handful of three-finger banjo innovators) to an eclectic, daring, flashy, jazzy, and innovative technique that marked him as a master of the instrument.

His flamboyance was well balanced by Red Smiley's lovely, smooth lead voice. This was also a departure from the bluegrass music that had gone before. Smiley's sincere, affable, relaxed vocal approach was quite different from the High Lonesome Sound of singers like Monroe and Stanley. Reno and Smiley's King recordings were blessed with songs of remarkably consistent high quality; and many of these have become bluegrass standards.

Red Smiley and Don Reno split up in the 1960s. Deteriorating health kept the genial Smiley in semiretirement until his death in 1972. Don Reno has continued on with a succession of partners and bands, continuing to bring both high entertainment and musical adventurousness to stages all across America.

THE OSBORNE BROTHERS

Sonny and Bob Osborne were among the first to "modernize" bluegrass, electrifying their instruments and recording a great many mainstream country songs with Nashville studio musicians. Still, their appeal to the hardcore bluegrass fans lay in Bob Osborne's astonishing, powerful tenor voice; in their instrumental virtuosity and innovation (Bob on mandolin, Sonny on banjo); and in their refinement of crystalline three-part harmony singing in bluegrass, an art which had tended to be haphazard at best before the arrival of these two Kentuckians in the late 1950s.

They recorded prolifically for Decca/MCA in the 1960s, and much of their material is still available. They currently record for CMH, and Rounder has released a couple of reissue albums of their very earliest material. They have been, and still are, both very outspoken and influential in shaping the course of modern bluegrass, and their recording of the now ubiquitous "Rocky Top" in 1968 made the song a standard.

JIM AND JESSE

The McReynolds brothers, Jim and Jesse, are two amiable Virginia gentlemen who brought the close-harmony, brother-duet style of old time country music into modern bluegrass music. This is a style that few other than family members ever master, for it demands that the singers phrase their notes as one, breathe as one, and keep the same tone qualities in their voices as they sing. Instrumentalists admire the duo as well, because of Jesse's astounding crosspicking mandolin style that emphasizes upstrokes on the strings and reverse finger rolls like Earl Scruggs's banjo style does. Another pickers' attraction is the fact that a succession of excellent banjo players have passed through the team's band, The Virginia Boys.

Jim was born in 1927, Jesse in 1929. They began their professional musical career as very young men, performing initially as an old-time duet. They began recording in the 1950s for Capitol, then switched to Epic and Columbia, where they enjoyed their greatest commercial success. Reissues of these performances can still sometimes be found.

Like many bluegrass artists, they currently record for CMH. Their sound today mixes straight-ahead, no-frills bluegrass music with commercial country elements. Jim and Jesse continue to prosper on The Grand Ole Opry each week, and on the bluegrass festival circuit in the summer.

RICKY SKAGGS

With the longterm, steady growth of an audience eclectic enough to appreciate and enjoy all forms of country music—from the Carter Family to Bob Wills to Carl Perkins to Rodney Crowell—it should come as no surprise that a young performer should eventually come along to shape all these sounds into a music of his own, both fresh and yet strongly traditional.

Skaggs has revolutionized country music by reacquainting it with its own past. Although he came from a bluegrass background, his love of all of country's root styles has led him at various times to record old-time brother-duet music, rockabilly, and western swing. In all of these cases he has emphasized sharp, tight instrumental playing; uncomplicated production;

simple, crisp rhythm tracks; and a grounding in acoustic instruments. He sings in a pure, mountain style that recalls Bill Monroe as well as some of Nashville's commercial country singers. Practically alone among bluegrass-based artists he has won the support and enthusiasm of traditionalists as well as from the modern country music industry.

Born in Cordell, Kentucky, in 1954, Rick was a child prodigy on a variety of bluegrass instruments, and indeed went on the road with Ralph Stanley at the age of 15. During his late teens and early twenties he toured with a variety of bluegrass bands, including the Country Gentlemen, J.D. Crowe's New South, and his own group, Boone Creek. In 1977 he joined Emmylou Harris's band, both contributing heavily to her sound and learning from those at the leading edge of the commercial music business. His own successful albums and singles for Epic followed, including a #1 song "Crying My Heart Out Over You," a contemporary update of a 1959 Flatt & Scruggs hit.

SELECTED RECORDINGS

- Bill Monroe
16 All-Time Greatest Hits *Columbia Records CS-1065*
- Bill Monroe
Master of Bluegrass *MCA Records 5214*

The numbers compiled on the Columbia album are the ones that brought Monroe immortality. The original versions of "Molly and Tenbrooks," "Blue Moon of Kentucky," "Will You Be Loving Another Man," "Footprints In the Snow," and other now-standard bluegrass songs are offered on this reissue. These are the seminal Bill Monroe recordings; thus, they are bluegrass music's foundation. There are many albums called *Bill Monroe's Greatest Hits,* but this is the one that contains his work with his best Blue Grass Boys band, the one that invented the music in the 1940s. This album defines bluegrass.

As if to demonstrate that neither he nor the music he loves has become moribund, Monroe released a dazzling demonstration of his instrumental abilities in 1981. Recorded during the sunset of his fabulous musical career, the LP nonetheless shines brightly. The overall tone of *Master of Bluegrass* is almost classical and reverent. The record's stately instrumental passages reflect the dignity of Monroe as few other releases have. It is a fine example of matured, aged-in-wood bluegrass.

- Flatt & Scruggs
Golden Era *Rounder Records 05*

Earl Scruggs's revolutionary banjo style was nearly

as important as Monroe's mandolin playing, heart-felt singing, and musical vision in creating the bluegrass sound. Using this record, compare Scruggs's finger picking with the earlier frailing banjo styles of Uncle Dave Macon or Grandpa Jones to see how dramatically he transformed the instrument. As revealed on this reissue, Lester Flatt's contributions as a vocalist and songwriter were major ones in the history of bluegrass music. Together, Flatt & Scruggs were unbeatable. *Golden Era* stands out as a definitive collection because it contains the performances that brought them country music fame long before *Bonnie and Clyde* or *The Beverly Hillbillies.* Bear in mind, however, that almost any Flatt & Scruggs album is worth getting.

● The Stanley Brothers
16 Greatest Hits *Starday/Gusto 3033*
● The Stanley Brothers
The Columbia Sessions, 1949–1950
Rounder Records 09
Carter and Ralph Stanley sang with the voices of hillbilly harmony angels. They created some time-less bluegrass melodies, and their musicianship is still widely admired today. Ask many bluegrass enthusiasts who the most moving musicians in the field have been and The Stanley Brothers's name will be a common reply. The Columbia recordings on the Rounder LP show them at their earliest, when they were still close to Monroe's pioneering style. Their King records, collected on the Starday/Gusto package, showcase them at the peak of their powers.

● Reno & Smiley
The Best of Reno & Smiley *Starday/Gusto 961*
"I Know You're Married But I Love You Still," "I Wouldn't Change You If I Could," "Freight Train Boogie," and "Money, Marbles and Chalk" are among the titles popularized by this superlative bluegrass act. These tunes, and the eight others on this reissue, make for an essential bluegrass collection in any country music library. The songs indicate that although the duo was a banjo-guitar combination like Flatt & Scruggs, they were capable of reaching beyond strict bluegrass numbers for their repertoire, and their finest moments together are preserved on this bit of vinyl.

● The Osborne Brothers
The Best of the Osborne Brothers
MCA Records 2-4086 (two-record set)
The traditional elements of a bluegrass band—mandolin, banjo, and piercing tenor vocals—are

present, but there's something much more here. The Osborne Brothers knew how to translate blue-grass music's essential appeal into commercial terms. They made hit singles. And even if they had done nothing but popularize "Ruby Are You Mad At Your Man" and "Rocky Top," their place in country music history would be assured. Those perform-ances are on this double album, as are many of the others that made them the pioneers of the so-called Newgrass movement. These are the numbers that helped move bluegrass from its grounding in old-time string band music into the modern Nashville world of electrified instruments, contemporary songwriting, and flashy performance style.

● Jim and Jesse
The Jim & Jesse Story
CMH Records 9022 (two-record set)
Jim & Jesse McReynolds are universally accepted as a solid bluegrass act. This is deceptive, however. During their long recording career they have been produced by such Nashville Sound stalwarts as Billy Sherrill, Jerry Kennedy, Frank Jones, Jimmy Bowen, and Larry Butler. They have frequently reached well beyond bluegrass boundaries for material, and have sung everything from "Snowbird" to trucker songs to honky-tonk laments to Chuck Berry numbers on records. Jesse's highly complex ("Stone Country") mandolin playing and the pair's Deep-South vocals have transformed all the parts of this catholic reper-toire into a coherent body of work that somehow remains in the bluegrass tradition. This album dem-onstrates their distinctive sound.

● Ricky Skaggs
Sweet Temptation *Sugar Hill Records SH-3706*
● Ricky Skaggs
Waitin' For the Sun To Shine *Epic Records FE-37193*
Skaggs, too, is embraced by the bluegrass commu-nity although he has moved beyond a bluegrass base. *Sweet Temptation,* with its swing passages and honky-tonk overtones, was his first LP that showed where he was headed. He maintained an acoustic sound on that effort, but was clearly mov-ing in a more commercial direction. His Epic album confirmed his desire to enter the mainstream coun-try marketplace. On it he revived Flatt & Scruggs's "Crying My Heart Out Over You" and "Don't Get Above Your Raising," and The Stanley Brothers's "If That's the Way You Feel," but there were songs from contemporary Nashville songwriters, from Merle Travis, and from Webb Pierce as well. Blue-grass or not, both albums were masterpieces.

Chapter Four

Depression Era Radio

There is no question that radio was the major force in country music in the 1930s. The Depression made the purchase of record players—and, indeed, records themselves at 75¢—a luxury far out of the reach of much of the country music's audience, but radio (once the set was purchased) was free. And the airwaves were jammed with country music, particularly in the dawning hours and at noon. On Saturday nights barn dance shows were broadcast from Nashville to Hollywood, from Shreveport to Minneapolis, from Atlanta to Chicago, and in St. Louis, Des Moines, Cincinnati, New York, and Wheeling. So it happened that radio "made" a great many stars; indeed, virtually every country music star emerging in that decade owed a great deal of success to radio, and a few, whose styles do not fall neatly into categories such as western swing, are profiled here.

It was not long before transcribed shows—like today's taped broadcasts—made their appearance, presenting a live-sounding show on a mammoth sixteen-inch disc. Several such programs have been reissued by smaller labels (most notable among them Charlie Monroe and his Kentucky Pardners on County, and the Sons of the Pioneers, who probably made more transcribed shows than anyone else, on JEMF). These shows are a particular joy, for they provide the otherwise unobtainable feel of live radio as it was in its heyday.

Of course, somewhere along the way somebody discovered it was cheaper and easier to play records over the air—the format which dominates (some would say strangles) American radio today—and a great era slipped away. It lives on today only on a few local stations, and in the one successful survivor, the Grand Ole Opry. Still, taped and syndicated radio shows like *Live From the Lone Star Cafe* and *Silver Eagle* demonstrate that the feel of live performance on radio can be a contemporary experience, though these are a far cry from the homey, folksy shows dominated by strange ads for Moc-O-Tan Tonic or baby chicks which dominated the 1930s and, to a lesser degree, the 1940s. Fortunately, much of this music, and a few of the actual radio shows, have been preserved, allowing us to share in this extraordinary era in American country music.

THE DELMORE BROTHERS

Alton (1908-1964) and Rabon (1910-1952) Delmore were two north Alabama farm boys who created a gentle, warm duet sound redolent of the red hill country of their birth. Their early sound was whisper-soft, featuring the somewhat rare combination of Rabon's lead tenor guitar and Alton's rhythm guitar, a host of fine original songs, many minor classics like "Brown's Ferry Blues," "When It's Time For the Whippoorwill To Sing," "Nashville Blues," and others. Their recording career began with Columbia in 1931, and with their six-year (1932-1938) stint with the Grand Ole Opry, though their finest work of this era was captured on their Victor sides.

They became one of the first country groups to investigate the increasingly popular boogie style in the 1940s, and though this was a radical shift in style, they achieved a second wave of popularity. Among their most popular records, recorded for King, were *Freight Train Boogie* and *Blues Stay Away From Me* (a trio with harmonica player Wayne Raney), a top five hit of 1949. Yet it was at this same time that they recorded some of country music's loveliest gospel music for King as part of the Brown's Ferry Four which also included Grandpa Jones and Merle Travis. Their recording career came to a close with Rabe's death, of cancer, in 1952.

On first listening their sound may seem too laid back, not intense enough; however, you must remember this kind of singing was a genuine novelty in its day—only recently had the advent of the radio made soft singing a possibility. Then, too, much of their appeal lay in their close harmony, and in the fresh and simple yet advanced musicality of their songs.

THE BLUE SKY BOYS

Bill and Earl Bolick were just 16 and 18 when they first recorded for Victor in 1936. Their mandolin-guitar duet singing formation was patterned after the Monroe Brothers (and, to a lesser extent, such duet teams as Mac and Bob, Karl and Harty, and the Delmore Brothers), but their sound was delightfully unique, and among the loveliest in American traditional music.

Their songs were often slow, many were ballads of British origin; and their gentle, resonant harmony expressed them with subtlety and beauty. Theirs is a sound evocative of the finest and most dignified music to emanate from the western Carolina highlands whence they came.

Both young men served long stretches in World War II, and resumed their career for a few years afterward before leaving professional music in 1951. They have reunited sporadically for festival and recording since then; both remain the quiet country gentlemen their records suggest.

The Bolicks have many devoted fans among old time music lovers, and it is our great good fortune that several fine reissues of their RCA material are still in print. It would be hard to top the Blue Sky Boys as an introduction to the best of rural music of the 1930s.

THE MONROE BROTHERS

As hinted at in the bluegrass section, the Monroe Brothers were one of country music's hottest acts in their brief (1934-1938) professional career.

Charlie (1903-1975) was a charming man, outgoing and friendly, a fine singer and a strong guitarist who was the model for many a later bluegrasser. Bill was shy and introspective, but spoke through his music, both in the clear intensity of his tenor voice and in the remarkable speed, clarity, daring, and thought with which he played his mandolin; he revolutionized the use of that instrument, previously used for lightly brushed rhythm or gentle solos.

Their music was aggressive, challenging, yet full of fun, and even nearly fifty years later it is easy to see why contemporary record buyers and radio listeners found it exhilarating; it is a delight not to be missed in the music of the 1930s.

Charlie continued with a fine country band, the Kentucky Pardners (a couple of excellent reissues of this band can be found on Country Records) for more than a dozen years after the Monroe Brothers split in 1938, eventually retiring to rural western Kentucky and making limited festival appearances late in his life. Bill, of course, went on to father bluegrass music, and continues as that style's reigning monarch.

The Monroe Brothers' closeness with bluegrass music should not, however, obscure the superb old-time music they played in the 1930s; it was unique and original and entirely its own.

LULU BELLE AND SCOTTY

Husband-wife teams have long been a staple of country music; one of the earliest and most popular was Lulu Belle and Scotty, regulars on *The National Barn Dance* from 1933-1958.

Lulu Belle was born Myrtle Eleanor Cooper in Boone, North Carolina, in 1913. Active musically as a teenager, she auditioned for the National Barn Dance in Chicago in 1932, and immediately became one of the stars of the show. She teamed with a very young Red Foley from time to time, then with another new cast member, Scott "Skyland Scotty" Wiseman (1909-1981), whose career had begun in 1927. They courted and married, and spent a long career sustained on their smooth duet sound and on Scotty's songwriting, which produced such standards as "Mountain Dew," (co-written with Bascomb Lamar Lunsford), "Remember Me," "Brown Mountain Light," and their biggest hit, "Have I Told You Lately That I Love You?".

In their years on the Barn Dance they recorded prolifically (for Conqueror, Vocalion, Okeh, Columbia, Vogue, Bluebird, Mercury, London, and Starday) and filmed several movies as well. Later they moved into television in Chicago, having a daily show over WNBQ from 1949-1957. Scotty began working toward a master's degree in educaton during the 1950s, and when they bowed out of the performing limelight in 1958, they retired to North Carolina, where Scotty became involved in teaching and Lulu Belle in politics, doing a couple of terms in the state legislature.

Their fine songs, their sweet harmony, and their homey image all contributed to a lasting success; sad to say their music has not endured as well as some of their contemporaries via reissues, which is a shame, for they represented a great picture of mainstream country music of their era.

PATSY MONTANA

Patsy Montana was one of the first women to be independently successful in country music. Not a member of a duet, nor part of a family act, she was a solo female star, a true pioneer. Patsy was the first woman in country music to have a million seller, 1935s "I Want To Be a Cowboy's Sweetheart."

Her country roots run deep. She was born Ruby Blevins on October 30, 1912, near Hot Springs, Arkansas. As the only girl in a family of ten boys she was raised a tomboy, and this may have made her later image as a cowgirl easy for her to adopt. She grew up hearing old-time country music, and even as a child began developing the powerful yodel that would make her famous. While still in her teens she won a talent contest singing a Jimmie Rodgers tune, "My Mother Was a Lady." After moving to California to live with an older brother, she continued to impress people with the songs of her idol, Rodgers. By this time her skills as a fiddler and guitarist were developing rapidly, since she appeared frequently on western radio shows. She adopted her stage name and the cowgirl clothes that went with it, so by the time she came back home from California she was "Patsy Montana, Montana's Yodelling Cowgirl."

During a guest appearance on Shreveport's KWKH Louisiana Hayride she was discovered by Jimmie Davis, who used her as a harmony singer and fiddler on his records in 1932. The following year Montana travelled to Chicago to audition for the girl-singer slot in The Kentucky Ramblers band on *The National Barn Dance.* The band was composed of Floyd "Salty" Holmes (guitar, tenor vocals), Shelby "Tex" Atchison (fiddle), Jack Taylor (bass), and Charles "Chick" Hurt (mandolin). In deference to their new member's established western image, they renamed themselves The Prairie Ramblers. Together, Patsy Montana and this extremely talented quartet became one of the hottest groups of the time. From 1933 to 1949 they produced consistently exciting music that was a blend of old-time string band music and the swing dance music that was getting America dancing. They often combined lively fiddling, blue yodels, and swinging polka rhythms in the same number. The result was an irresistible hybrid.

In addition, Patsy pioneered an independent woman's image in country music. Her lyrics (she wrote many of the songs) frequently emphasized freedom and independence in conjunction with companionship and love.

Montana continued to pursue a musical career while she married and raised a family. As the Depression wore on, she performed tirelessly on radio, records, and shows. In the 1940s she had her own national radio show and appeared in several films. She retains her popularity overseas to this day, and usually makes one European tour each year. Her warm and good-humored independence has withstood the test of time, appealing to audiences for over 50 years.

SELECTED RECORDINGS

- The Delmore Brothers

Brown's Ferry Blues *County Records 402*

- The Delmore Brothers

The Best of The Delmore Brothers
Starday/Gusto Records

Beneath the quiet, somewhat dignified musical presentation the Delmores offer on *Brown's Ferry Blues* is a soulfulness that becomes mesmerizing with repeated listenings. Their warm soft voices are complemented beautifully by their rippling guitars. Indeed, the brothers were unique among Depression-era brother-duet acts in that they were as creative as instrumentalists as they were as harmony singers. "Big River Blues," "Til the Roses Bloom Again," "Fugitive's Lament," "The Nashville Blues," and "Brown's Ferry Blues" all demonstrate this amply.

Delmore Brothers music divides roughly into two distinct periods. Their country-blues period was during the 1930s. In the 1950s they emerged again as proponents of a country-boogie style. In both of these periods, they produced fascinating, complex, black-influenced country duets. The Starday album anthologizes the later phase. It, too, is a joy.

- The Blue Sky Boys

Sunny Side of Life *Rounder Records 1006*

- The Blue Sky Boys

Presenting The Blue Sky Boys *JEMF Records 104*

The Blue Sky Boys, as showcased on these two fine records, specialized in plain-spoken, evocative, simple music that looked backward to The Carter Family and forward to later brother duets like The Louvin Brothers and Everly Brothers. These two brothers are a quintessential example of how members of the same family can sound singing perfectly together. Their twin-like voices harmonize eloquently, weaving in and out of one another in perfectly timed alternating phrases. The overall effect is of sublime musical poetry. The Rounder LP contains some of their best-known performances. The JEMF reissue brings their obscure Capitol album of folk songs back into print.

- The Monroe Brothers

Feast Here Tonight
RCA Bluebird AMX-2-5510 (two-record set)

The Depression era saw the rise of many, many brother duet acts in country music. This should not be read as a sign of sameness in music, however, for each of the prominent brother duets brought something unique and special to the art form. The Blue

Sky Boys had stunning harmonies and intricate vocal arrangements. The Delmores had a languid, soft, bluesy quality and some outstanding guitar playing. The Monroe Brothers had tension, drive, and intensity in their voices. Bill's mandolin playing was fast and clean. Charlie was an expert showman. The two hit first with "What Would You Give In Exchange?" in 1936, and followed it with memorable performances of "He Will Set Your Fields On Fire," "Have a Feast Here Tonight," "Drifting Too Far From the Shore," "On That Old Gospel Ship," and "Roll In My Sweet Baby's Arms." These and many more were compiled by RCA for this outstanding package.

- Lulu Belle & Scotty Wiseman
Sweethearts of Country Music
Starday Records SD-206
Although no reissue album of Lulu Belle & Scotty's old 78s has yet appeared, this LP the couple made for Starday in the 1960s recaptures what was best about their simple, affecting style. The elements that made them great were still there as they grew older. In fact, Lulu Belle's sense of pitch arguably improved with time. And the songs are still classics. Versions of their immortal "Have I Told You Lately That I Love You," "Remember Me," and "Mountain Dew" were all recorded for this Starday package; and all survived the test of time and the change in instrumentation from the original versions well. This record is characterized by the warmth and wit that made Lulu Belle the queen of the most important country radio show of the Depression, *The National Barn Dance.* Indeed, it's easy to hear why she was voted the most popular female radio entertainer in the United States for two years in a row in the 1930s.

- Patsy Montana
Patsy Montana Sings Her Original Hits From the West
Cattle Records (Germany) LP-13
Cattle Records has released several anthologies of Patsy and The Prairie Ramblers' work. All are simply delightful. This one contains most of the biggest hits; another emphasizes the group's earliest recorded work; and a third focuses on comic and western themes. A performance like "Swing Time Cowgirl" demonstrates just how *hot* the band was with swing material. "I Wanna Be a Cowboy's Sweetheart" lets Montana's flashy yodeling come through. "Back On Montana Plains" and "Ridin' Old Paint" contain one ear-tickling instrumental lick after another; while "Goodnight, Soldier" illustrates that Patsy was at home with ballad selections

as well as her more familiar uptempo numbers. If an American record label ever unleashes a Patsy Montana & The Prairie Ramblers reissue, the lady's place in country music history will doubtless be elevated; for this is an act that brilliantly bridged the gap between what was best in old-time string band music and what was exciting about hillbilly jazz and western swing.

OTHER RECOMMENDED DEPRESSION-ERA RADIO STARS' RECORDINGS:

● The Bailes Brothers
Early Radio Favorites, Vol. 1
Old Homestead Records OCHS-109
The Bailes group was yet another of the brother acts that came to the fore during the Depression. Although they did not attain mass radio popularity until the 1940s, their style, outlook, and songs belong essentially to the previous decade. They wrote and popularized country standards like "Dust On the Bible," "I Want To Be Loved (But Only By You)," and "Oh So Many Years." Recorded radio versions of all are on this LP.

● The Girls of the Golden West
The Girls of the Golden West
Sonyatone Records STR-202
Stars of *The National Barn Dance* projected a characteristic homey warmth, a pleasant, dulcet quality that is easily heard in the voices of Lulu Belle & Scotty and Patsy Montana. Even more in this vein were sisters Millie and Dolly Good, The Girls of the Golden West. Their projection of WLS's gentle, rosy, fireside ambiance made them the most popular female duet in country music history. Sonyatone has made 16 of their soothing, close-harmony performances available again.

Chapter Five

Singing Cowboys

Though he should always be viewed with affection, the singing cowboy is surely one of the 1930s most peculiar cultural creations. Taken only loosely from history (some cowboys, like some sailors, miners, and loggers, occasionally sang on the job) and melded with the unsubtle heroism of the dime novel, Tom Mix film, and the Buffalo Bill Wild West Show, this film and musical genre became surprisingly popular throughout the nation, and indeed the world, during the Depression.

Though it began with Ken Maynard and John Wayne (in his earliest roles as "Singin' Sandy" Wayne's voice was dubbed by big band vocalist Smith Ballew), it was Gene Autry who galvanized the style with his open good looks, affable, innocent, shy personality, and sincere, downhome singing style. He was followed by a large posse of singing cowboys, as every studio rushed to emulate his success. Many fine singers—George Houston, Fred Scott, Dick Foran—came from the professional stage, and left little mark; the cowboys with backgrounds in country singing—Tex Ritter, Roy Rogers, Ray Whitley, Jimmy Wakely, Rex Allen—tended to have longer, more successful careers in this style which, above all, demanded sincerity (sometimes, in the face of the action on screen, a heroic act in itself) from its performers.

The style was popular for a number of years, though after World War II its popularity diminished: "Cool Water," "Riders In The Sky," and "High Noon" are the only western tunes to achieve large success in the postwar era, and most of the singing cowboys found their record successes in love songs and laments in the country vein.

The film genre lasted longer, into the 1950s, but it too slowly faded from sight, and only in very recent years has much attention been paid to this lovely and lyrical style, which though far removed from its folk roots gave us an uplifting picture of a grand and noble west, of breathtaking vistas and independent, unfettered men who roamed them. It gave us great performers, like Autry and Ritter and the Sons of the Pioneers, and it gave us traditional music's finest poet, Bob Nolan, but most of all it gave us a powerful, romantic self-image which is unique in American music, and powerful beyond music.

GENE AUTRY

Orvon Gene Autry was born on a small ranch in Tioga Springs, Texas in 1907, though he grew up near Ravia, Oklahoma. Enthralled by performing from his youth, he spent a summer with a medicine show during high school, but upon graduation settled down to a job as a relief telegrapher.

A chance encounter with Will Rogers, who heard him singing on the job one day, fired young Autry's ambition, and he took some vacation time to travel to New York early in 1929, a trip which produced little interest. He went home, practiced diligently, and was far better received upon his return to New York late that year, beginning a series of recordings for a number of labels.

His early sound was virtually indistinguishable from Jimmie Rodgers (not everyone remembers how fine a yodeler Autry was in his prime), but he began to shift toward sentimental mountain ballads, and scored his first hit in this style, a duet (with Jimmy Long, his former boss on the Frisco Road) called "That Silver Haired Daddy Of Mine."

He became a popular entertainer on radio—first on KVOO in Tulsa, then on WLS in Chicago, where he plunged headlong into cowboy song and image, coming up with his first western hit in 1933, "The Yellow Rose of Texas." It was at this time he was tried out by Mascot pictures, appearing to sing two songs in a Ken Maynard film *In Old Santa Fe* (1934), the first of over one hundred films he would make.

His portrayal of the shy, likeable cowboy with the million-dollar smile and pleasant country voice caught on immediately, and he quickly became one of the most popular film stars in America. In addition, he continued to be one of Columbia Records biggest sellers for over fifteen years, and starred in the long running *Melody Ranch* radio show. In addition, he entered the television marketplace early, producing

**Gene Autry shaped the image of the singing
cowboy in his music and movies.**

over 100 Gene Autry shows as well as several others.
With the decline of interest in westerns and western
music, and his own growing business empire, he gradually left the performing arena to concentrate on his
widespread businesses, continuing through today.

His influence on the music of the era and those that
followed is immense, not only in the performers he
inspired but in the wholesome, heroic, good-guy image he gave to rural music. He was *the* major country
music star of his era, and though much of his accompaniment sounds dated, his voice retains that sun-
warmed sparkle that made many of his songs among
the most popular of his time.

Some of his innumerable hits were "Left My Gal In
The Mountains" (1930), "Moonlight and Skies" (1932),
"There's An Empty Cot In The Bunk House Tonight"
(1933), "The Last Roundup" (1934), "Tumbling Tum-
bleweeds" (1935), "Mexicali Rose" (1936), "There's A
Gold Mine In The Sky" (1938), "Take Me Back To My
Boots And Saddle" (1938), "Back In The Saddle
Again" (1939), "South of the Border" (1940), "You Are
My Sunshine" (1941), "Be Honest With Me" (1941),
"At Mail Call Today" (1945), "Have I Told You Lately
That I Love You?" (1946), "Here Comes Santa Claus"
(1947), "Rudolph, The Red Nosed Reindeer" (1949),
"Peter Cottontail" (1950) and "Blue Canadian
Rockies" (1950).

ROY ROGERS

Born Leonard Franklin Slye on November 5, 1912, the young man who would become known as The King of the Cowboys grew up in and around Cincinnati, Ohio before heading to California in 1930. With his fine, clear voice and spectacular yodeling ability, he was able to find employment in a number of Southern California string bands—most modeled on the tremendously popular Beverly Hillbillies—before forming his own with tenor Tim Spencer and baritone Bob Nolan. They called themselves the Pioneer Trio at first, later changing that to the Sons of the Pioneers, and made musical history.

Their brief years together were memorable, for they brought trio harmony singing to undreamed of heights in country music, and all three were fine songwriters who helped shape a whole vision of the West. Leonard Slye left the group in 1937 (though they continued to record with him and appear in his films off and on from that day to the present) to pursue a career in films. First as Dick Weston, then as Roy Rogers, he became one of the most popular film stars of his time. Indeed, through his films and popular television series, he truly "raised a whole generation of kids," as he is fond of saying.

He recorded a good bit of material, first for Columbia, and then over a more than two decade span with RCA. Though many of his sides are brilliant, he never found great commercial success on record, despite the magnitude of his film and television career. Only recently have some of his best early sides been reissued (usually as part of Sons of The Pioneers packages); one longs for more of his genial sound.

He and his wife Dale Evans maintain a light personal appearance and television schedule to this day; a recent appearance on *The Muppet Show* proved that his remarkable yodeling abilities have not diminished, though he now approaches his 70th birthday.

TEX RITTER

Woodward Maurice Ritter was born to a prominent Texas family in Panola County in 1905. From his youth he was interested in authentic cowboy song, and studied it at the University of Texas (though his major was pre-law) in Austin, even spending a year in law school at Northwestern before abandoning that career for one on the Broadway stage.

He appeared in a number of productions—most notably *Green Grow The Lilacs* in 1930—and appeared on a number of radio shows, including the New

York based WHN Barn Dance, before heading for Hollywood in 1936, filming *Song of the Gringo,* the first of over 60 films he was to make for several differnt studios up until 1945.

Though he quickly became one of the most popular film stars in America, his records for ARC (1934) and Decca (1935–1939) did not overwhelm the buying public. Upon joining Capitol Records in 1942, however, he began a long string of hits which made him one of country music's biggest selling artists of the 1940s. His unusual and distinctive voice projected character and honesty, and among his many hits were "Jingle, Jangle, Jingle" (1942), "Jealous Heart" (1944), "There's A New Moon Over My Shoulder" (1944), "I'm Wasting My Tears On You" (1945), "You Two Timed Me One Time Too Often" (1945), "Rye Whiskey" (1945), "Green Grow The Lilacs" (1945), "High Noon" (1952), "The Wayward Wind" (1956), and "I Dreamed Of A Hillbilly Heaven" (1961).

As the singing cowboy era began to fade, Tex took to endless touring, becoming one of the most travelled entertainers in America. He also appeared frequently on television (especially as co-host of *Town Hall Party* in LA), and eventually moved to Nashville in 1965, where he became a member of the Grand Ole Opry.

A tireless campaigner for the preservation of western and country music history, he remained active on tour and in Nashville until his sudden death, of a heart attack, in 1974.

For the neophyte Tex Ritter's completely unique voice may take some getting used to. As a child I loved it dearly, while my parents thought it ridiculous; I felt then, and still feel, a sense of theater, a sense of humor, a sense of integrity and honesty in that voice, and I suspect those very things were the key to his long and successful career.

JIMMY WAKELY

Handsome, smooth-singing Jimmy Wakely was a natural singing cowboy star, seemingly born for the part. Born in Arkansas in 1914, he migrated to Oklahoma as a child, turning to music at an early age. He formed a Sons of the Pioneers-style western trio with Scotty Harrell and another great country songwriter, Johnny Bond, in 1937 in Oklahoma City, and in 1940 moved to Hollywood to become part of Gene Autry's radio and touring show.

He immediately began recording ("Too Late" was an early hit) and appearing in small roles in films before landing a starring series in 1945; he ultimately appeared in over fifty films, and in 1948 was voted fourth most popular western film actor. His warm, rich, smooth voice, reminiscent of Bing Crosby's, seemed a natural for recording success, but he did not hit his stride until signing with Capitol in the later 1940s, hitting first with "One Has My Name, The Other Has My Heart" in 1948, then with the million-selling "Slipping Around" (one of country music's classic duets) with Margaret Whiting in 1949.

He remained popular on record, in person, and on radio via his CBS radio show throughout the 1950s, and maintains a limited appearance schedule to this day, though much of his energy is devoted to his own record label, Shasta, which is not surprisingly the best place to obtain a great deal of fine Jimmy Wakely material long out of print (though much of it may seem too pop-oriented for purists), as well as good live recordings of other western artists such as Merle Travis, the Sons of the Pioneers, and others.

SONS OF THE PIONEERS

The long and complex history of the Sons of the Pioneers began in October of 1933 when Len Slye— later to be known as Roy Rogers—coerced two fellow southern California musicians to get back into the music business they'd quit during the Depression. This they did, forming a group they called the Pioneer Trio, consisting of Slye, Bob Nolan (1908–1980), and Tim Spencer (1908–1974).

The Sons of the Pioneers practically defined the classic sound of western music.

Nolan's legendary gift for songwriting was already well in evidence, for he brought to the group songs like "Tumbling Tumbleweeds," "I Follow The Stream,"

"Way Out There," and others. Tim Spencer immediately began to add a great many fine songs, though his most popular compositions were not written until the 1940s: "Room Full of Roses," "The Everlasting Hills of Oklahoma," and others. Nolan sang baritone and played bass, Spencer sang tenor, and Slye sang lead, did the fancy yodeling, played guitar, and wrote several fine songs himself.

The group was greatly strengthened in 1934 with the addition of Hugh Farr (1903–1980), a superb Texas fiddler, and shortly thereafter by his guitar-playing brother Karl (1909–1961); they formally became The Sons of the Pioneers that year as well. The middle 1930s were active years for them as they began a long series of musical support roles in films, and recorded many fine sides for Columbia and Decca, and began their long series of recorded radio transcriptions.

In 1936 Tim Spencer left briefly, replaced by Lloyd Perryman (1917–1977), a 19 year old with a glorious voice, and Pat Brady (1914–1972) was added to play bass and do comedy when Leonard Slye became Roy Rogers and went on to film stardom at Republic. Spencer then rejoined, singing lead as he was to do throughout the remainder of his career.

World War II took two members, Perryman and Brady, and they were replaced by tenor Ken Carson and bassist Shug Fisher. This version provided RCA with some of the Pioneers' most popular records: "Cool Water," "Cowboy Camp Meeting," and "The Everlasting Hills of Oklahoma." Perryman and Brady returned after the war, but major changes occurred in 1949, when Tim Spencer left the Pioneers for good, followed in a few months by Bob Nolan.

Spencer was replaced by a great singer, Ken Curtis (now far better known for his portrayal of Festus on *Gunsmoke*), and Nolan by similar-sounding Tommy Doss, a mainstay of the Pioneer sound through 1963; it was at this time that Perryman took over leadership of the group, and he was to remain trail boss until his death in 1977. It is Dale Warren—who replaced Ken Curtis in 1953—who has since led the Pioneers on their still successful career. The rock years were hard on all of western music, but thanks largely to Perryman's determination the Pioneers weathered them, despite the loss of Hugh Farr in 1958 and the death of Karl Farr in 1961. A great many singers and musicians have passed through the group—including Billy Armstrong, Rome Johnson, Deuce Spriggins, and a returning Pat Brady—in the past decades, and the current group, now recording for the first time in several years, features Warren, Luther Nallie, and Rusty Richards as the vocal trio, with Roy Lanham on guitar and Dale Morris on fiddle.

The Pioneers' influence on country music has been doubly strong; not only did they bring the art of trio singing (and yodeling) to a peak yet unsurpassed, virtually defining the substyle western music in doing so, but through the efforts of Nolan and Spencer they brought music of undreamed subtlety, beauty, and poetry to a wide audience. We are fortunate a great many Pioneers reissues exist; listening to their music is exceptionally rewarding.

RIDERS IN THE SKY

Western music does not dominate the country scene as it once did, but it's not a dead country music genre either. Riders In The Sky is proof of that. This young Nashville trio revives many singing cowboy standards, but also creates much excellent original material that draws on the same spirit and inspiration. The group is a regular feature on today's Grand Ole Opry.

The elements that make up the Riders' style are those which have delighted western music fans for years: spectacular yodeling, smooth close-harmony singing, and instrumental flash. The three are capable of switching instantly from a cowboy ballad to a hot, jazzy fiddle instrumental. An added feature is the band's rambunctious comic sensibility which gives it the wit, verve, and panache that raise it considerably above standard country fare.

Formed in 1978, Riders In The Sky has risen rapidly to a place of prominence in country music. More importantly, the trio is reinvigorating one of the country's most fascinating styles.

SELECTED RECORDINGS
ANTHOLOGIES:
Legendary Songs Of The Old West
Columbia Special Products P4-15542
(four-record set)
Master discographer Bob Pinson compiled this essential four-record set for sale through Publisher's Central Bureau. It may be hard to obtain, but it's worth it: there are 48 performances, many of them unissued classics, from the rough-hewn 1930 "Home On The Range" of Ken Maynard to Tex Ritter's unreleased 1933 sides, to the Sons of the Pioneers' metaphysical "Song of the Bandit" to Roy Rogers's delicately intricate yodeling "Cowboy Night Herding Song." Some of the song selection seems *discographimaniacal!* to the point of

perversity—three versions of "Seven Years With The Wrong Woman," a pedestrian song at best, is a bit much—but most performances have both historic significance and musical inspiration, and there are some truly great cuts here: Autry's original "Back In The Saddle Again," Bob Wills's "Cherokee Maiden," and the Sons of the Pioneers' "Hold That Critter Down."

INDIVIDUAL PERFORMERS:
● Gene Autry
Country Music Hall of Fame Album
Columbia Records CS 1035
● Gene Autry
Gene Autry *Columbia Historic Edition FC 37465*
From "Back In the Saddle Again" to "Mexicali Rose" to "Take Me Back To My Boots and Saddle," the Gene Autry songs collected on the *Hall of Fame* album are truly pieces of Americana. They are also among the titles that were our most important sing-ing cowboy's greatest hits. There are more interest-ing albums for the scholar and musicologist, but this longstanding favorite compilation is still the best all-around Autry buy. It is worth pointing out, however, that most of these tracks are 1946–1948 re-recordings of his classics.

The Columbia Historic Edition package takes a different tack. Autry was adept at much more than just western numbers. He handled romantic pop love songs, heartache country ballads, and close-harmony Pioneers-type tunes, as well as his solo singing cowboy stuff. This reissue samples each of those styles, including as it does "Don't Fence Me In," "It Makes No Difference Now," and "Tumbling Tumbleweeds." As a bonus, a previously unissued version of one of Autry's better-known numbers, "There's a New Moon Over My Shoulder," is also included. On all these, Autry's warm, crooning tenor still sounds as wholesome as milk-and-cookies on a Saturday morning.

● Roy Rogers
The Best of Roy Rogers *RCA Camden ACL-1-0953(e)*
It is really astonishing that the most awesome singer of all the country cowboy stars has never had a major reissue devoted to his contribution. This set compiles some of his movie material, and varies widely in quality. There are some rather banal, forgettable numbers here, but some gems as well. Roy possessed the most beautiful singing voice and most impressive yodelling ability of all the major singing cowboys. This record is merely a reminder of those considerable musical abilities.

● Tex Ritter
American Legend
Capitol Records SKC-11241 (three-record set)
By contrast, this boxed set of records is one of the most loving tributes ever devoted to an American singer. It spans Ritter's career completely, offering early pure-cowboy performances, show tunes, and Nashville Sound hits like "I Dreamed of a Hillbilly Heaven." The accompanying notes add to the pleasure. It's a somewhat expensive set, but surely worth the price to anyone with memories of Saturday matinee shoot-em-ups, anyone with a sense of country music history, or anyone who falls under the still-strong sway of singing-cowboy music.

● Sons of the Pioneers
Sons of the Pioneers
CBS Columbia Historical Edition FC-37439
This fine set of 12 sides dates from 1937, and features six previously unreleased performances, though some are alternate takes and some are from sessions cut by Roy Rogers with the Pioneers as a backup band, after he had formally left the group. The Farr Brothers are in fine form, and the seldom heard vocal trio of Nolan, Rogers, and Perryman is absolutely excellent. Particularly outstanding are some great Nolan songs ("Song of the Bandit," "At the Rainbow's End," "Hold That Critter Down," "The Touch of God's Hand") and a couple of exemplary yodels by Roy Rogers. Short but germane and informative liner notes by Fred Goodwin and outstanding cover art make this a fine package; its main flaw, as a whole, is the lack of more recognizable material and the conspicuous absence of any vocal solos by lyrical Lloyd Perryman.

● Riders In The Sky
Three On the Trail *Rounder Records 0102*
Bob Nolan, who wrote the affectionate liner notes to the Riders' debut album before his death, is widely regarded as the poet laureate of western music. These three disciples, however, have followed in the master's footsteps admirably. Newly composed numbers like the lyrical "Blue Montana Skies," the cowboy-comical "That's How the Yodel Was Born," the deeply touching "Cowboy Song," the rhythmic "Here Comes the Santa Fe," and the jazzy "Blue Bonnet Lady" faithfully evoke the classic singing cowboy era while bringing its imagery up to date. The trio's expert handling of such oft-sung standards as "Ghost Riders In The Sky," "Don't Fence Me In," and "When Payday Rolls Around" makes them fresh again. Take the lovable western music sound

and bring it to modern recording techniques and studios and you have Riders In The Sky.

OTHER RECOMMENDED SINGING-COWBOY RECORDINGS:

● The Farr Brothers
Texas Crapshooter *JEMF Records 107*

Hugh (fiddle) and Karl (guitar) Farr were the instrumental foundation for The Sons of the Pioneers, a group justly celebrated for its songwriters and harmony singers. On their own they recorded a series of extremely lively instrumentals for radio broadcast. Recorded in the mid-1930s, these hot little numbers were part of Pioneers Standard Transcription radio shows. Their reissue was a boon to all fiddle tune lovers.

● Marty Robbins
Gunfighter Ballads and Trail Songs
Columbia Records CS-8158

This album introduced the new cowboy classics "Big Iron" and "El Paso." Many modern country stars have paid tribute to the singing cowboys of yore, but only Marty Robbins brought the tradition back into mainstream popular acceptance. His silver voice, acoustic accompaniment, and keen ear for commerciality made this the biggest selling western-themed LP in history. Besides his own award-winning compositions, Robbins tipped his hat to authentic cowboy folk song ("Strawberry Roan," "Utah Carol") and to the golden-era western material ("Cool Water," "Down In the Little Green Valley"). The harmony singers he introduced on this record (the composers of his popular "Running Gun") later gained fame as Tompall & the Glaser Brothers.

Chapter Six

Western Swing

The Depression did funny things to the American psyche; nowhere is this better seen than in music. Among the hardest hit were the working people and farmers, who were country music's biggest audience. Across the small towns of America some people embraced the escapism of the singing cowboy; in the southeast they listened to the plaintive songs of mother and home; in the southwest, they danced their troubles away.

Though discophiles may tend to forget it, western swing was dance music first and foremost, evolving from small Saturday night living room get-togethers to huge 18 and 20 piece dance bands playing to huge audiences.

Western swing was one of country music's most creative forms in an era of creative forms; yet more than any other it was also the most adaptive, borrowing freely and cheerfully from big band, blues, Dixieland, from southern hoedowns and ballads, from lonely cowboy laments to the hottest pop swing of the era. It was a determinedly eclectic music, dedicated to dancing to such a degree that couples two-stepped merrily to the insistent beat though the lyrics might be tales of heartache and woe.

It also attracted some of country music's finest jazz musicians of the day, making each performance a new and exciting experience for the musically minded; one wonders, in retrospect, why this unique style with its great good feel and dynamic musicianship took so long to be revived.

Its heyday was the Depression, and its king was indisputably Bob Wills, who started as a fiddler at dances around Fort Worth. Then with his band the Texas Playboys, he created much of the style, sound, and repertoire that define the style. Many others followed and contributed much, but western swing passed out of vogue after World War II, its sphere of influence growing smaller and smaller, retreating to the Texas-Oklahoma region in which it was born.

Merle Haggard's magnificent album "A Tribute To The Best Damn Fiddle Player In The World," and the appearance of a zany young band called Asleep At The Wheel rekindled the interest of a new generation in the style, and though it does not scorch the national charts, there is a large, enthusiastic following once again for this jazzy style, and, consequently, a great many reissued performances by Wills, Cooley, and many other influential performers and masters of western swing.

MILTON BROWN

Always cited as one of the founders of western swing, Milton Brown led the band that trained many of the genre's finest musicians. Born in Stephenville, Texas in 1903, he worked both as a salesman and a policeman before meeting Bob Wills in 1931. The Light Crust Doughboys combo they formed recorded for Victor as the Forth Worth Doughboys in 1932. That Dallas recording session is sometimes cited as the birth of western swing.

Brown and Wills split shortly thereafter, each forming his own outfit; Milton Brown's musical Brownies were a cheerful outfit unafraid to tackle any style, and particularly receptive to jazz and swing, propelled by the dazzling steel guitar of Bob Dunn, and Brown's own swinging tenor voice. They recorded quite a few sides for Decca, and were only beginning to achieve their measure of popularity as western swing became popular when Brown was killed in an auto accident in 1936.

Brown's pioneering role in western swing was caught on these early sides; and one can only speculate on what he might have achieved had he lived.

BOB WILLS

The son of a fine old-time fiddler, James Robert Wills was born in Limestone County, Texas, in 1905. Music remained a constant in an erratic childhood and young adulthood (which saw him take up occupations like farmer, preacher, and barber), and by 1929 he had taken it up full time forming a band first known by the name of one sponsor—Alladin's Laddies—and then another: the Light Crust Doughboys.

Bob, his brother Johnny Lee, and vocalist Tommy Duncan split from the extremely popular Doughboys in 1933, forming Bob Wills and his Playboys, a name later changed to Texas Playboys the following year, when they began their successful and creative eight-year stay in Tulsa.

It was during these Tulsa years that the style called western swing was established and refined: based on the fiddle—solo and harmony—and the rhythm guitar, with the steel guitar, horns, drums, piano, and reeds developing an exciting, jazzy hybrid of country, jazz, blues, swing, and a touch of mariachi and Cajun thrown in for good measure. It was driving, romantic, exciting dance music, and it was in this Tulsa era that Wills achieved his greatest record successes: "Spanish Two Step" (1936), "Steel Guitar Rag" (1937), "Maiden's Prayer" (1938), "San Antonio Rose" (1939), "New San Antonio Rose" (1940), "Take Me Back To Tulsa" (1941), "Home In San Antone" (1943) and many other classics. His film career began then as well, beginning in 1940 with *Take Me Back To Oklahoma,* starring Tex Ritter; he was to appear in some 26 musical westerns during the war years.

During this time a host of creative musicians came and went: Leon McAuliffe on steel guitar, Eldon Shamblin on electric guitar, Al Stricklin on piano, Louis Tierney, Joe Holley, and dozens of other fiddlers, Smokey Dacus on drums, Joe Ferguson and Laura Lee Owens on vocals, Cameron Hill and Jimmy Wyble on guitars, and a host of others. However, after the war the national mood seemed to shift away from big dance bands in general, and though Bob Wills continued to thrive—in Oklahoma, California, and Texas—for many years, the handwriting was on the wall for western swing. Bob eventually was forced to make cutback after cutback in the size of the big band (22 pieces at its largest) of which he was so proud, although even through the 1950s he performed and recorded a great deal of excellent music. Despite failing health in the 1960s he stayed busy, and was able to record as late as December of 1973 before succumbing to complications from a series of strokes on May 13, 1975.

Although western swing was first and foremost a dance music, Bob and the Texas Playboys were for years a vital, innovative force in country music, for their willingness to experiment and to amalgamate disparate musical forms made them one of the most creative—and certainly one of the most versatile—bands in America. Uninhibited by real or imagined musical strictures, Bob Wills conducted a lifelong musical experiment in western swing.

A recent resurgence in interest in western swing has caused the flowering of many reissues of Wills material, from bootleg to small label to major label. It is music easily approached and easily enjoyed, and gives an authentic feeling for the southwest which is as accurate today as it was when Bob Wills and his daring young friends defined the style 40 and 50 years ago.

SPADE COOLEY

The self-proclaimed King of Western Swing was born Donnell C. Cooley in Grand, Oklahoma, in 1910; the son and grandson of fiddle players, he quickly became an expert on the instrument, and moved to the West Coast, appearing in small roles in films (though he starred in two extremely obscure singing cowboy westerns) and both playing in and leading dance bands. He eventually led the West Coast's most popular western dance band, which at times included up to 20 musicians, complete with harpist.

His sound was smoother and more calculated than many other western swing outfits, very swinging and highlighted by Cooley's own dynamic stage presence. An additional plus was Tex Williams's smooth baritone, often paired (as in their huge 1945 hit "Shame On You") with the country tenor of Smokey Rogers.

Cooley's smooth pop sound helped him weather western swing's declining years; unfortunately much of his musical contribution has been overshadowed by his prison term spent for murdering his wife in 1961. He died of a heart attack shortly following his release in 1969.

ASLEEP AT THE WHEEL

Ray Benson, Leroy Preston, and Lucky Oceans began, like many other college kids, forming a small country band with which to try to duplicate the sound of the great truck-driving country music of the 1940s and 1950s. They quickly fell under the spell of Bob Wills and western swing, and soon expanded to a nine and ten piece band which played great western swing, yet could and would also boogie, jump, and sing tender love ballads as well. Both a show band and a dance band, they quickly caught the favor of a young generation, and introduced the powerful sound of western swing to this whole new audience.

A great many talented musicians and singers have passed through the band—Chris O'Connell, Floyd Domino, Link Davis Jr. Mary Ann Price—and at present only Ray Benson remains of the original band. Still, their many albums are still available, and every live performance is an adventure in itself. Plagued by shifting personnel, their future is never sure, but in bringing two generations of western swing lovers to a common source, they have assured themselves of a place in history.

SELECTED RECORDINGS

- **Various Artists**

Okeh Western Swing Ok-37324

CBS Records, in recent years at least, has proved to be the most innovative and responsible major label in terms of reissues of their classic material, be it via leasing—as they have done with classic bluegrass, to Rounder and County—or coming up with their own labels, the Columbia Historic Editions, or reviving their classic Okeh label.

The Okeh revival at present is an experiment; one fervently hopes it will be kept alive. Among the first five sets, one is devoted exclusively to western swing, and it is a gem, including 28 cuts from 1928–1950. One side is exclusively devoted to Bob Wills, and several other Western swing pioneers are included: Roy Newman, Hank Penny, Adolf Hofner, Spade Cooley, and others. John Morthland's superb liner notes trace western swing from its jazz and vaudeville (especially fine is Emmet Miller's *Lovesick Blues*) roots as well as its beginnings in barn dances, and there are excellent photos as well.

All in all it is a remarkable set, good history and good entertainment at the same time.

INDIVIDUAL PERFORMERS:

- **Milton Brown**

Country & Western Dance-O-Rama

Western Records 1001

This is that recently revived LP format, the ten-inch mini-album. It is a faithful reproduction of Brown's lone Decca album of the early-1950s, and as such may prove to be nearly as sought-after a collector's item as the original record itself. It was Western Records' first effort, and if it is any indication of the kinds of things the firm intends to do in the future, deserves every country fan's support. It is at once a document of Milton Brown's pioneering western swing work, and a souvenir that brings back the look and feel of an early country LP.

- **Bob Wills and his Texas Playboys**

The Bob Wills Anthology *Columbia KG 32416*

This album remains the model for first class reissue work, complete with striking cover art, and well-written (by Bill Ivey) and researched (by Bob Pinson) liner notes and discographical information.

The 24 songs on this double set begin with "Osage Stomp," from Wills's first Columbia session in 1935, and continue on through his final 1946 session for the label, with "Brain Cloudy Blues." In between are an excellent selection of the hits ("New San Antonio Rose," "Steel Guitar Rag," "Take Me Back To Tulsa"), and underexposed sides, including real gems like the previously unreleased "Mississippi Delta Blues."

Wills's gamy and fascinating mixture of fiddle tunes, jazz, pop, big band, country, and Dixieland is nowhere more apparent; the feel of western swing at its peak is captured neatly and joyfully.

● Spade Cooley
Spade Cooley *Columbia Historic Edition FC 37467*
This long-overdue reissue on "The King Of Western Swing" is one of the delights of Columbia's recent reissue project, and this collection contains many of Cooley's best known tunes, including "Detour," "Crazy 'Cause I Love You," "Hide Your Face," the pop-swing instrumental "Swinging The Devil's Dream," and his hit record of 1945, "Shame On You."

Most of the material is delightful, though it has neither the intensity nor the sense of joyful spontaneity that makes Bob Wills's music often an adventure. The high spots are Tex Williams's authoritative baritone and the legendary Joaquin Murphy's breathtaking steel guitar playing. On the other hand Smokey Rogers's tenor vocals, while accurate, have a surprisingly corny feel for so smart a band.

Attractive cover art and insightful though not detailed liner notes by Jimmy Wakely help make this an attractive package, but perhaps not the one to begin a western swing collection with.

● Asleep At The Wheel
Wheelin' and Dealin' *Capitol Records*
Asleep At The Wheel's Ray Benson and country superstar Merle Haggard can take most of the credit for reviving western swing music in the 1970s. They reacquainted young audiences with the music of such eclectic, innovative experimenters of the 1940s as Bob Wills and Moon Mullican. Like Haggard, Asleep At The Wheel drew its inspiration from a variety of styles, of which western swing was the most ear-catching; thus, their identification as a western swing unit.

The group's first album, on United Artists, contained the most western swing material, but it has been long unavailable. Of the Wheel's subsequent Capitol discs, *Texas Gold, Served Live,* and this LP present the biggest doses of this lively music. The revivals of "Route 66" and "Miles and Miles of Texas" on the *Wheelin' and Dealin'* album brought them special praise from western swing fans; and they used veteran swing pickers like Tiny Moore and Eldon Shamblin on "Blues For Dixie" on this record. On later efforts various group members turned toward boogie-woogie, blues, honky-tonk, and jazz for inspiration. Benson, himself, has continued to reach toward the interesting, obscure, and new, rather than be stuck with the label of "western swing revivalist" forever.

OTHER RECOMMENDED WESTERN SWING RECORDINGS:
● Billy Jack Wills
Billy Jack Wills & His Western Swing Band
Western 2002
Billy Jack has lived in the shadow of his more famous brothers Bob and Johnnie Lee, but he made music as jumpin' as anything they ever did. He is generally thought of as the lyricist of the classic "Faded Love" and as a member of The Texas Playboys. This LP demonstrates his considerable ability as a bandleader in his own right.

The onrushing, sweeping notes of teenage prodigy Vance Terry's steel guitar gave Billy Jack's group the classic big band sound of the Super Chief wooshing across the midwestern plains. That high-powered, diesel-driven sound surprisingly came from a small, seven-piece band. Another surprise is the fact that this music was made well after the heyday of western swing. Billy Jack Wills did these radio performances in the early 1950s.

The continuing enthusiasm for country's jazz stepchild has led to the reissue of some of western swing's lesser known bands. In this case, country/jazz lovers should be glad.

● Hank Penny & His Radio Cowboys
Tobacco State Swing *Rambler 103*
By contrast with the full-bodied Wills sound, this is small combo jazz. Sheldon Bennett's fiddle skips jauntily along, weaving in and out of melody merrily. That deft, light-fingered styling is the hallmark of Hank Penny's Radio Cowboy band.

Tracks reissued here like "Hesitation Blues," "Sweet Talkin' Mama," "Won't You Ride In My Little Red Wagon," and "Hot Time Mama" indicate that Hank Penny had one of the hottest little bands of his era. His breezy, relaxed vocals combined with the snappy picking of his sidemen made for music that is inescapably country, yet unmistakably jazz.

Chapter Seven

Country Music: 1940s

The 1940s were the end of the age of innocence in country music. During this decade the form made the transition from rural music with regional appeal to big-money polished entertainment. It moved from being acoustic-based to being electrified. It moved from amateur to professional. It became modern.

Old-time music encompassed string bands (like The Skillet Lickers), brother duets (like the Blue Sky Boys), family harmony groups (like The Carter Family), folksingers (like Bradley Kincaid), and rambling songsters or bluesmen (like Jimmie Rodgers). By the end of the 1940s all of these types of performers had faded.

Singing cowboy music prospered because of film and television in the 1950s. Western swing maintained popularity because it married country music to the pop music, big band sound. But they survived the 1940s just barely. By the late 1950s they, too, had died.

Nearly all the performers who thrived in the 1940s straddled the old and the new. All were firmly grounded in old-time music styles of the 1930s, but all had the ability to adapt to the new commercial reality. The modern country song publishing business was born in Nashville during this decade, as was the recording studio scene that concentrated, centralized, and homogenized country music. The Grand Ole Opry took over country radio leadership from Chicago's National Barn Dance during this same period, so its stars assumed new luster. The popularity of groups and instrumentalists waned. In their place, charismatic vocal soloists took the spotlight.

It was the beginning of the star system in country music. It was the start of country songwriting as we know it today. It was the dawn of a multimillion dollar country music industry.

ROY ACUFF

Roy Claxton Acuff was born September 15, 1903; in Maynardville, Tennessee, to a family with a rich musical heritage. Although music remained an integral part of his life as a youth, his main interest was athletics, and having won some thirteen letters in high school sports, he was set on a career as a professional baseball player. A series of setbacks after a severe sunstroke ruled that out, however, and he turned to practicing the fiddle while recuperating.

Roy Acuff, "King of Country Music," has sold more than 30 million records.

He began a professional career in 1932, joining a medicine show; he has often maintained that this experience molded his later style, for here he learned showmanship and his earnest, forceful singing style. He formed his own group the following year, and was first recorded by the American Record Company in 1936; by 1938 he was a member of the Grand Ole Opry, and his career skyrocketed with such hits as "The Great Speckle Bird" (1937), "Wabash Cannonball" (1938), "Wreck On The Highway" (1942), "Fireball Mail" (1942), "Night Train To Memphis" (1943), "Low and Lonely" (1943) and many more. Among his other accomplishments were hosting the network portion of the Grand Ole Opry, starring in eight films, and running for the governorship of Tennessee in 1948. He continues to perform on the Grand Ole Opry to this day, having mellowed into its dignified and gracious elder statesman, and a minor 1974 hit called "Back In The Country" gave Acuff the honor, at the age of 70, of being the oldest performer to have a record "on the charts" in the history of popular music.

Acuff's sound is both evocative of the Tennessee hills from which he came, and yet unique to him. His sturdy, earnest, sincere approach to a song is the key to his success—though he is quick to jump into an uptempo novelty tune lest things begin to drag. Another Acuff hallmark has been superb fiddling, and the lilting Dobro (acoustic steel guitar) of Beecher Kirby, aka "Bashful Brother Oswald," now a 40-year veteran of Acuff's Smokey Mountain Boys.

This is pure country music, unalloyed and unashamed, and not only was it phenomenally popular in its day—strongly influencing Hank Williams and a host of others—but it still speaks to us today. Successful pop songwriter turned country writer and publisher Fred Rose claimed he never fully understood country music or its appeal until he saw Roy Acuff on the Opry one night, his eyes brimming with tears as he sang the mournful dying-child ballad "Tying The Leaves So They Won't Fall Down." His point is well taken.

GRANDPA JONES

Grandpa is much more than the brash banjo-playing buffoon seen on television's *Hee Haw* each week. He is a one-man encyclopedia of sentimental Victorian songs, folk melodies, medicine-show routines, traditional instrumental tunes, and gospel song treasures. He is the last remaining exponent of an old-time show business style that has nearly faded from the American scene. He is a national treasure.

His exuberant, shouting, joyous style comes from years on stages from Boston to San Francisco. A veteran of radio barn dance programs and multi-artist packaged country shows, his sincerity and professionalism let him make the transition to television.

Louis Marshall Jones, his real name, was born in Kentucky in 1913, but when he was a teenager his family moved to Akron, Ohio. There he won a talent contest and garnered a slot on local radio. Discovered by Bradley Kincaid, he went on the road with the beloved folk singer and absorbed his traditional repertoire. While on the radio as part of Kincaid's show, fans wrote in asking his age saying that he sounded old. Thus, at age 22 he became "Grandpa" on stage.

He changed instruments from banjo to guitar in the 1930s after he saw some of the legendary Cousin

Emmy's showmanship with the instrument. He adopted many of her moves, featuring high kicks, exaggerated arm motions, reared-back posture, and held-high frailing solos. He plays the banjo with his whole body.

After considerable success at Wheeling, West Virginia's WWVA *Jamboree* Grandpa took his act to Cincinnati's WLW *Boone Country Jamboree.* There he met his fiddling wife Ramona, another supremely accomplished old-time musician.

Together, they moved to Nashville and The Grand Ole Opry in 1946. Since then, Jones's star has soared higher and higher; for he made the sounds of the past palatable to audiences of the present.

MERLE TRAVIS

Along with Maybelle Carter, Chet Atkins, and very few others, Merle Travis is one of the most influential guitarists in country music history. His complex finger-picking style is the link between the folk guitarists of his native Kentucky and the commercial country style popularized by Chet Atkins and Nashville's studio players.

He is equally renowned as a songwriter. His "16 Tons," "Dark As a Dungeon," "Smoke! Smoke! Smoke! (That Cigarette)," and "So Round, So Firm, So Fully Packed" all became major hits.

In the late 1940s and early 1950s he was a highly successful recording star himself, with the likes of "No Vacancy" and "Divorce Me C.O.D." He starred in films and became noted as a cartoonist, too.

Travis was born in 1917 and grew up quite poor. His schooling ended before high school, but his instrumental talent got him working in country radio bands by the mid-1930s.

By the end of the 1940s he was famous in two of the three major country recording centers of the time, Cincinnati and Los Angeles. By the close of the following decade he was famed in Nashville as well.

RED FOLEY

Foley is the perfect example of the transition made by country performers during the 1940s. He initially performed in the 1930s as part of the string band The Cumberland Ridge Runners on WLS's National Barn Dance.

His straight-from-the-heart vocal delivery made him a solo star at WLW in Cincinnati beginning in 1937. Two years later he became the first country star to have a national network radio show.

By the 1940s he was a Nashville star; and as the decade wore on he became smoother and smoother as a balladeer. His soothing tones were perfect for the songs that Music City tunesmiths were hammering out by the mid-1950s.

He parlayed his huge success as a recording artist into television stardom on *The Ozark Jubilee* and *Mr. Smith Goes To Washington* national network series. In the 1960s he made a successful transition to gospel music stardom because of his way with hymns and songs of praise. By this time his vocals were nearly indistinguishable from dozens of nightclub crooners.

Foley was born in Berea, Kentucky, June 17, 1910. He died after a concert in Fort Wayne, Indiana on September 19, 1968, one year after he had been elected to The Country Music Hall of Fame.

PEE WEE KING

Just as Bob Wills and the western swing bandleaders adapted big band jazz to a country format, so Pee Wee King took the kind of music made by society orchestras and rode to country success with it. His secret was melody. His Golden West Cowboys didn't swing like The Texas Playboys. His vocals were pleasant but unexceptional. But he had a piano player named Redd Stewart who wrote irresistible commercial tunes.

Stewart and King are responsible for "Slow Poke," "Bonaparte's Retreat," "You Belong To Me," "Tennessee Tango," and "The Tennessee Waltz," one of the most popular country songs of all time.

King was a Milwaukee bandleader and accordionist who was discovered by Gene Autry in 1934. His easygoing style matched that of America's honey-voiced singing cowboy. From there he quickly made his way to Nashville and The Grand Ole Opry.

Once in Nashville he developed a large roadshow operation. In the course of his tours he developed the careers of Eddy Arnold, Minnie Pearl, and Ernest Tubb, all of whom became country superstars in their own right. King also was featured in films and on television shows. By the late 1940s Pee Wee's compositions were becoming successful in the pop music field. He was a pioneer in bringing Nashville songs to national attention.

MOLLY O'DAY

There are more than a few people, her ex-producer Arthur Satherley among them, who feel that Molly O'Day is the greatest female country singer ever. Her appealing, earnest style—not unlike Roy Acuff's and

Wilma Lee Cooper's—is the epitome of the mountain sound of country music of the 1940s.

She was born LaVerne Williamson in Pike County, Kentucky, on July 9, 1923, and embarked on a professional career in the summer of 1939. She married fellow bandmember Lynn Davis in 1941, and the two set out on their own for a number of years, touring throughout the Southeast. Her first session for Columbia, in December of 1946, produced many of her classics: "Tramp On The Street," "Six More Miles," "Black Sheep Returned To The Fold," and many others, followed on later sessions by "Poor Ellen Smith," "The First Fall of Snow," and "Matthew Twenty-Four."

In 1950 she and Lynn began recording only sacred material for Columbia—the content had already been high—and when Molly contracted tuberculosis in 1952, she and Lynn both left their musical careers to become ministers in the Church of God, careers which they both follow to this day.

There is no question that Molly O'Day quit performing and recording well before her prime; she certainly had all the talent and appeal to become country music's first really great and really popular woman singer.

SELECTED RECORDINGS

● Roy Acuff
Greatest Hits *Columbia CS 1034*
When Roy joined The Grand Ole Opry in 1938 the show's cast was dominated by old-time string bands. He became the program's first real solo singing star.

Acuff had a superb, hot-picking, high-energy acoustic band called the Smokey Mountain Boys that matched his electrifying, exortative, emotional singing lick for lick. They were an instant success and were on national radio in just a couple of years. The release of a few spinetingling Columbia 78s cemented his stardom. He has reigned ever since as The King of Country Music.

It's too bad that there is no currently-available LP containing all the great original Acuff singles. If contemporary fans could hear the original versions of "Great Speckle Bird," "Wabash Cannonball," "The Precious Jewel," "Night Train To Memphis," "Fire Ball Mail," "Wreck On the Highway," "My Tears Don't Show," "Pins and Needles," and the rest of his history-making performances again, they'd understand why he's considered one of country's most important vocal stylists.

This Columbia album collects a few of them, but its "Wabash Cannonball" is not the original; and the entire record is in simulated stereo. There are two out-of-print Harmony budget discs that are worth tracking down *(Great Speckle Bird* and *Night Train To Memphis),* but avoid the so-called *Greatest Hits* packages on Capitol and Elektra.

● Grandpa Jones
The Grandpa Jones Story *CMH 9007*
● Grandpa Jones
Family Album *CMH 9015*
The original versions of Grandpa's best-known songs (such as "Eight More Miles To Louisville," "Mountain Dew," and "Ol' Rattler") are on Starday 3008. The gospel quartets he recorded with The Delmore Brothers and Merle Travis (as The Browns Ferry Four) are also highly recommended, on Starday 3017.

But Grandpa Jones has never really been a hitmaker. So it seems more important to emphasize the old man's ongoing function as a wellspring of old-time tunes and demonstrate his continuing musical vitality. These CMH records do that admirably.

They attempt to explain and encompass his huge repertoire and capture his expansive, open style on disc. All the historically important Jones numbers are here, as are many lesser known tunes. The second LP shows him in the family-singing setting with his beloved Ramona and their four musically gifted children, all of whom have taken to his old-time repertoire with gusto and musical excellence. Both records are accompanied by superb sets of liner notes that eloquently explain Grandpa Jones's musicological significance.

● Merle Travis
The Best of Merle Travis *Capitol SM-2662*
When Tennessee Ernie Ford made Travis's "16 Tons" into a worldwide hit in 1955, Merle's place in country music history was secure. By that time the songwriter had been a hitmaker himself for several years. All of those hits are in their clean, pure, original form on this fine Capitol LP.

And if Merle Travis is not the nation's greatest singer, his vocal limitations are more than made up for by his guitar prowess. He is in the elite company of Chet Atkins, Maybelle Carter, Les Paul, and Joe Maphis as a country musician's musician.

Enjoy him as a great songwriter, enjoy him as a relaxed natural song interpreter, or enjoy him as one of the great instrumentalists. In any case, you'll appreciate his election to The Country Music Hall of Fame.

● Red Foley
Red Foley Memories *Vocalion 73920*

● Kitty Wells & Red Foley
Kitty Wells & Red Foley's Golden Favorites *MCA 83*
There is an album called *The Red Foley Story* available from MCA; but it is a collection of his vocal tracks overlaid with strings and background singers to give it a "modern" sound. Foley's original versions are smooth enough. When he's loaded down with that sort of production, he sinks into blandness.

Red Foley Memories doesn't contain any of his big hits, but at least its songs are presented as they were originally heard. The earnestness, heart, and sincerity of the man's singing can be better appreciated this way.

One still-available collection that does contain hits is the compilation of Red Foley/Kitty Wells duets on MCA. Six of their finest early performances together are reissued as are three tender solos from each. "One By One," "As Long As I Live," and "Make Believe ('Til We Can Make It Come True)," the duo's biggest hits, are worth the price of the disc alone.

● Pee Wee King
The Best of Pee Wee King *Starday 965*
King is another Opry legend whose best performances are out of print. Pee Wee King and Redd Stewart, the creators of the most popular country song of all time, are perhaps the most shockingly overlooked country musicians of the 1940s. Until RCA reissues the original versions of their huge hits, this re-recording of them will have to do. There was an RCA Camden budget LP in 1971 called *Pee Wee King's Biggest Hits* that included "Bonaparte's Retreat," "Slow Poke," and "Tennessee Waltz." Find it if you can.

● Molly O'Day
A Sacred Collection *Old Homestead 101*
This album is all that remains of the meteoric, brief career of Molly O'Day. It brings together her classic gospel sides of the late 1940s.

Her repertoire, like that of her contemporaries Roy Acuff and Wilma Lee Cooper, was heavily laced with intensely devotional numbers and mournful yearning old-time tunes. Like those mountain performers of kindred spirit, she wailed her songs with open-throated urgency. The sound quality here is not the greatest, but O'Day's talent shines through every groove.

Chapter Eight
Honky-Tonk Music

"Honky-tonk" is at once a place, an attitude, and a musical style. The music was born in oilfield roadhouses of the 1940s where beer and blood flowed freely. It faced the modern world head-on with lyrics of infidelity, divorce, alcohol, work, and sex. As a style it incorporated steel guitars, drums, electric guitars, and raw emotional lead singing.

When you think of hard country music today, you think of the honky-tonk style. The whine of the steel guitar, the thump of drums, the slurred bluesy vocals, and the gutbucket emotions of cheatin'-and-drinkin' songs are now things we take for granted as ingredients of a mainstream country record. They are all characteristics of classic honky-tonk music, however, and this style did not always dominate as it does today.

The post-World War II era was a time of tremendous social upheaval in America. When country boys returned from overseas and country girls came home from the factories society was forever transformed. After the war romantic relationships became unstable, labor strikes mounted, the family dwindled in importance, and the divorce rate soared. America became a mobile, less homebound society and took on the rootless, restless quality it has retained.

This is when the honky-tonk assumed its importance as a social gathering place. Drinking and dancing were ways to blot out society's troubles.

The musical accompaniment to the raucous, rowdy behavior that resulted was usually the jukebox. These electric amplifiers of dance records soared in popularity between 1938 and 1948; and the honky-tonk was, in fact, sometimes called a juke joint. Only the glowing, multicolored jukebox had enough bass sound and volume to be heard over the din of the smoke-filled barroom. When live country music was brought into these places, the bands had to adjust their sound and style.

More than ever before, rhythm became important in country bands. The stand-up bass became common in honky-tonk bands, and a second guitar was frequently added for rhythmic punch. In time, small drum kits became common as well. Country music was forever after married to a beat. Thus, even when the words and music couldn't be heard above the noise level, the dance rhythm could be felt.

A honky-tonk singing style evolved as well. Honky-tonk singers went into unashamed vocal histrionics. Vocal cries became common. Slipped notes, bent phrases, and melodic curlicues attracted attention to the singers. They cried, wailed, moaned, and whined as never before. This was a style of showmanship previously unseen in country music.

The electric guitar was also adopted, but the instrument most closely identified with the honky-tonk sound is the steel guitar. Its piercing sound, wide emotional range, and loud electronic ability made it the most indispensable of all the honky-tonk musical elements.

Honky-tonk changed the substance of the country song, too. Church, mother, home, and sweetheart were jettisoned in favor of downbeat subjects that spoke of pain, despair, and anguish.

Unlike other country music substyles, honky-tonk music completely permeated the field. It was absorbed so fully into the country mainstream that today it is thought of as *the* historical tradition. When country musicians talk of returning to good old-fashioned country music today, they usually mean pure honky-tonk, not mountain music. And when most fans think of a country singing style, they think of the tear-in-the-beer wail of the honky-tonk singer.

ERNEST TUBB

Tall, lanky Ernest Tubb embodies the transition between simple, soft, old-time country music and the raw, harsh sounds of the modern era. Born in Crisp, Texas in 1914, Ernest idolized the music of Jimmie Rodgers from an early age. He was such a disciple that he sought out Rodgers's widow Carrie. Through her, he gained his first entry into show business.

Tubb's recordings in the 1930s were in direct imitation of his idol; but by 1941 his style had changed dramatically. His voice lowered from years playing in

Texas dives and dance halls, his band's instrumentation expanded and amplified, and his songwriting toughened, he scored a huge hit with the down-beat "Walking the Floor Over You."

He became a B-movie star and a Grand Ole Opry member on the strength of his to-the-point songs and homey drawl. "Two Glasses Joe," "Slippin' Around," "Blue Christmas," "Letters Have No Arms," and "You Nearly Lose Your Mind" polished his honky-tonk sound to perfection; and Ernest Tubb became one of the most consistent hit-makers of the 1950s and 1960s.

Tubb's seemingly bottomless voice may never have hit a true note, but there are few that can match it for expressiveness. Ernest slips on and off notes with seeming disregard for pitch, yet he maintains as powerful a sense of melody as he does a feeling for lyrics. Through his Texas Troubadours passed some of country music's finest instrumental stylists; and the band is widely regarded as having pioneered steel guitar sounds and electric guitar leads.

Although he was elected to The Country Music Hall of Fame in 1966, Ernest Tubb continues to perform well over 200 dates a year. From this wellspring flows the honky-tonk style.

HANK WILLIAMS

If Ernest Tubb defined honky-tonk's musical style, Hank Williams surely defined its lifestyle. The tragic whiskey- and drug-soaked life of Williams has been a pattern that country music's honky-tonkers have followed ever since.

Williams's humor and high life were contrasted with a Southern boy's deep sense of guilt and remorse. That is why his religious songs are every bit as effective as his cheatin'-and-sinnin' standards. In the voice of Hank Williams is the soul of Southern postwar America. In his songs are the desires and regrets of us all.

Unlike most of the honky-tonk pioneers, Williams was not a Texan. An Alabama native, he was born September 17, 1923. Twenty-nine years later he was dead of heart failure January 1, 1953. In the intervening years he became a country superstar and the most important singer/songwriter in Nashville history.

The sound of Hank Williams is the sound of raw emotionalism. His singing had cries and moans and choking breaks. His Drifting Cowboys band whined with steel guitar, thumped with stand-up bass, and jangled with rhythm guitar. His song lyrics ached with desire, yearned for lost love, winked with humor, or percolated with the pleasure of partying.

Hank Williams embodied the sound and the lifestyle of honky-tonk music.

It is a testament to his talent that the music of Hank Williams continues to sell like no other performer's of his generation. He was never crowned King of Country Music, but he is considered the king of the honky-tonk style to this day.

LEFTY FRIZZELL

Frizzell possessed one of the most heart-stopping voices in country music history. His vocal influence on modern country music is incalculable. Although not regarded as such at the time of his death in 1975, he is now being recognized as the most influential country vocal stylist of the honky-tonk genre. For an all-too-brief time in the early 1950s he rivalled even the great Hank Williams in popularity.

William Orville "Lefty" Frizzell was born in Corsicana, Texas March 31, 1928, the son of an itinerant oil driller. He acquired his nickname as a teenage Golden Gloves boxing contender. Also as a teenager, he began playing the rough honky-tonks of Dallas and Waco. Like so many performers of his generation, he was deeply influenced by the music of Jimmie Rodgers.

He was first recorded by a recording studio engineer named Jim Beck in Dallas. With their simple accompaniment, down-to-earth topics, and Lefty's arresting vocal phrasing, these performances made him a star.

By 1951 he was king of the country popularity charts. That year he had four songs in the top-ten simultaneously, a feat never since duplicated by anyone. In the late 1950s and early 1960s he enjoyed a career resurgence by recording the saga songs that Nashville was then specializing in. Lefty's "Long Black Veil" (1959) and "Saginaw Michigan" (1964) were memorable contributions to this shortlived vogue. Then, sadly, he went into a career slump that lasted for the rest of his life.

Frizzell remains one of the most individual, unique stylists in country history. That is why music lovers continue to discover him today.

RAY PRICE

Price's Cherokee Cowboys band was formed from the remnants of Hank Williams's Drifting Cowboys organization, so Ray's music had a direct link to the apex of the honky-tonk style. After Williams's death in 1953, Price rose to take his place as a consistent honky-tonk hitmaker.

Like most of the classic honky-tonk performers, Ray Price was an East Texan. Born on January 12, 1926, he began performing on Dallas radio when he was in his early 20s. He was deeply influenced by Hank Williams even before the two met and became friends; and his early recordings clearly demonstrate his debt to Williams's style.

Ray's #1 hits began coming in 1956 with "Crazy Arms." Nearly all the ingredients of pure honky-tonk were present on this disc: Price's Hank-like vocal rides atop a steady thumping bass beat with a fiddle sawing away in support in the background. The steel guitar was added by the time of his next smash success, "Heartaches By the Number," in 1959. The slur of the steel perfectly meshed with the song's theme of lost love and ruined romance, the stock-in-trade of the honky-tonk moaner.

In the 1960s, Ray Price switched styles to become a smooth-voiced balladeer. Lush, string-laden arrangements replaced the simpler honky-tonk sound. His early records still remain true classics of their era.

GEORGE JONES

Any country music fan will tell you George Jones is the greatest living honky-tonk singer.

Jones is almost as well-known for his drinking excesses and irresponsible behavior as he is for his music. "The Rolls Royce of Country Singers," as he is sometimes called, careens through life like a besotted old bluesman. Fans consistently forgive him, however; and disc jockeys eagerly await his every release. George Jones, more than any other modern country artist, has a life that mirrors his music. That honky-

tonk music is the white man's blues is no better illustrated than in the person of George Jones.

He sings in an unearthly voice of after-hours bars,
wee-hours drug abuse, and back-alley rendezvous. He
lives, like Hank Williams did, in a world of titanic
overindulgence and schizophrenic mood sweeps. He
has squandered his ability and his money. And he is a
genius.

Yet another East Texan, George was born in Sara-
toga in 1931. He began as a Hank Williams imitator;
then scored a hit with his own emerging style in 1955.
By the mid-1960s he was touring incessantly; and it
was at this time that his pattern of wild, self-destructive
living began to imitate the lyrics of honky-tonk songs.

His personal and professional teaming with Tammy
Wynette, a superb vocalist capable of an aural teardrop in every note, brought him to mass acclaim in the
1970s. By the 1980s he had achieved even greater
acceptance and acclaim, despite the fact that the
divorce from Wynette had sent him into a nearly
psychotic tailspin. His honky-tonk artistry remains undimmed by time and personal misfortune.

WEBB PIERCE

Pierce was arguably the most electrified of the classic
honky-tonkers. His "Slowly" (1954) is said to be the
first country hit to feature the pedal steel guitar; the
slip-note piano style of Floyd Cramer was a part of his
band; and the guitar and voice of Faron Young were
also among Pierce's contributions to country culture.

Born in West Monroe, Louisiana in 1926, Webb
initially gained fame on the Louisiana Hayride, then a
training ground for The Grand Ole Opry. By 1955 he
was a member of the Opry itself, and was enjoying a
solid string of successes.

Pierce epitomized 1950s country music. His voice
had a nasal, authoritative sound that drove hard-luck
honky-tonk lyrics home with a vengeance. That barroom, whipped-dog, yell-of-pain "edge" in his music
made Webb Pierce a superstar from 1952 to 1962, but
that same quality made him sound dated to the pop-
oriented Nashville of the 1970s. He remains, however,
one of the most authentically "country" vocalists still
singing.

SELECTED RECORDINGS

- Ernest Tubb

The Ernest Tubb Story *MCA 2-4040 (two-record set)*
Tubb's humble sincerity and smiling gargoyle face
are the very essence of country stardom. His lacka-
daisical phrasing, drawling diction, and slurred

vocal notes are the very essence of honky-tonk singing.

"E.T.," as he's known to country fans throughout America, is something of an acquired taste for many listeners. On first hearing, he sounds as if has no concern for melody, and, at best, an eccentric sense of time. Subsequent listenings, however, make Ernest addictive. There is something simply charming about the way he slides up to notes—sometimes never even hitting them accurately—and about the way he urges on the eloquent little solos from his Texas Troubadours band.

Regrettably, Decca/MCA added strings and voices to his classic songs when it released this compilation LP during the height of the Nashville Sound era. There is a Rounder Records collection that has Tubb in his original musical setting, but it does not include many of his most famous songs, as this double-LP set does. Tubb's honky-tonk instrumentation may not survive on this slicked-up disc, but his inimitable voice still weaves its spell.

● Lefty Frizzell
Remembering . . . . the Greatest Hits of Lefty Frizzell
Columbia KC 33882
George Jones, Merle Haggard, John Anderson, John Conlee, Johnny Rodriguez, Willie Nelson, and dozens of other contemporary country performers openly acknowledge the stylistic influence of Lefty Frizzell. He is possibly the most imitated vocalist in modern country music. Frizzell's spinetingling off-the-beat phrasing, note curling, and bluesy-sweet quality make him one of country music's most absorbing, involving, innovative singers of all time.

His early recording sessions in Dallas captured the essence of his art in 1950–53. Lefty was joined by a tiny little honky-tonk band enlivened by the plinky-plunk piano playing of a Waco school teacher whom producer Don Law remembers only as "Madge." From these sessions emerged "If You've Got the Money, I've Got the Time," "I Love You a Thousand Ways," "Always Late," "Mom and Dad's Waltz," and "Give Me More, More, More (of Your Kisses)," all stone honky-tonk classics and all included in this compilation.

Once introduced to this magnificent master stylist, the honky-tonk student will also want to hear Rounder Records *Treasures Untold: The Early Recordings of Lefty Frizzell* and the Columbia Historic Edition set *Lefty Frizzell,* both of which also capture him at the peak of his powers.

Frizzell died in 1975 at age 47. Surprisingly, it took until 1982 for his contribution to win him a place in the Country Music Hall of Fame.

● Ray Price
Ray Price's Greatest Hits *Columbia CS 8866*
Recent initiates into country music fandom might be surprised to find Ray Price's name on a list of seminal honky-tonk performers. Today, he's known as a tuxedo-clad crooner of nightclub love songs. In the mid-1950s, however, Ray was the rival of Hank Williams, Lefty Frizzell, and Ernest Tubb as a honky-tonker. He and Williams were, in fact, room-mates in Nashville.

With his fine Cherokee Cowboys band, Price became a superior honky-tonk performer with the likes of "Heartaches By the Number," "I'll Be There," "Crazy Arms," "Release Me," and "City Lights." His instrumentation was always tight; and he was one of the most notable superstars to bring the steel guitar sound out front. Another trademark was Price's prominent use of fiddle licks.

Vocally, he was a different man back then. His voice broke frequently and he exuded wailing, white-man's soul. In the 1960s he lost that "edge," and dropped lower into his baritone range for the likes of "Danny Boy" and "For the Good Times."

Bear in mind that there are two Ray Prices. If you're a honky-tonk fan, seek out the earlier one.

● Hank Williams
24 of Hank Williams Greatest Hits
MGM SE-4755 (two-record set)
Only Jimmie Rodgers can claim as all-pervasive an influence as Hank Williams. If no other performer defines honky-tonk music to the general public, the sound of Hank Williams does.

The prolific singer/songwriter died before the age of 30, but his impact was so immense that it scarcely mattered that he had a hit-making career of only four years. "Your Cheatin' Heart," "I'm So Lonesome I Could Cry," "Cold, Cold Heart," "Kaw-Liga," "Lovesick Blues," "Jambalaya," "Hey, Good Lookin'," "I Can't Help It (If I'm Still In Love With You)," "Half as Much," "You Win Again," "Why Don't You Love Me (Like Ya Used To Do)," and "Take These Chains From My Heart" only scratch the surface of the man's genius.

His patented yodel effects and high, keening, nasal whine remain unequaled vocal sounds in country music. His Drifting Cowboys' lap steel guitar–dominated arrangements are still distinctive.

This double album set has most of his biggest records. Although the majority have been presented in their original forms, a few gussied-up tracks snuck through. As with virtually every other major stylist of his era, Hank Williams suffered under the strings-and-background-vocalists over-dubbing of The Nashville Sound during the 1960s. This LP and its follow-up, *24 More of Hank Williams Greatest Hits,* are mainly free of this kind of mutilation. Be extremely cautious in buying any other Hank Williams albums, however.

● George Jones
Greatest Hits *Mercury ML 8014*
Jones is the performer who brought honky-tonk music into the modern era. Since his hits began coming in the late 1950s he is a second generation honky-tonker. But, like most of the first generation performers, his musical roots are in post war Texas.

George's familiar clenched-teeth, throaty-slide, airy-whine singing is the envy of the country music world. His is an out-of-the-body voice that is almost frightening in its eloquence. What is even more eerie is the fact that it has been with him from the beginning and has intensified, not diminished, with age.

There is a huge amount of George Jones material to choose from. Fortunately, there is no such thing as a totally bad George Jones record, so the consumer can't go wrong. George's Starday LPs show him during his raw Texas beginnings. His Mercury records contain his big breakthrough hits. Although the Nashville Sound instrumentation on these is sometimes unsympathetic, the Mercury LPs defined his style. Many of his biggest hits are on the United Artists albums. Musicor Records (later re-released on RCA) had him during his longest sustained hit streak. The contemporary George Jones has been able to produce a very satisfying string of LPs for Epic Records.

The appeal of this Mercury collection is in the songs. The rockabilly-flavored "White Lightning," the aching ballad "Tender Years," and whiskey-soaked honky-tonk numbers like "Window Up Above" and "Color of the Blues" are all included.

● Webb Pierce
Best of Webb Pierce *MCA 2-4087*
Nasal voiced Webb is the person your city-slicker cousin is referring to when he says, "I can't stand the way country singers sound." Pierce could wail off-key, yet move the listener, like few others of his era.

His heyday was the 1950s, but he has continued to thrive as a live performer into the present. During the peak years, Pierce found some of the greatest country songs in history to record. "Wondering," "Slowly" (the first major country hit with an electric pedal steel guitar), "I Ain't Never," "There Stands the Glass," "Missing You," and "In the Jailhouse Now" are just a few of his immortal hits. These songs virtually define the mainstream country music of their era. Webb's sharpedged, whining delivery imprinted them in memory indelibly.

Put up, once again, with the violins that were added later. Some stylists are so distinctive they can withstand anything.

OTHER RECOMMENDED HONKY-TONK RECORDINGS:

- Floyd Tillman

The Best of Floyd Tillman *Columbia KC-34384*

Along with Ernest Tubb, the three pioneers of honky-tonk music in the 1940s were Ted Daffan ("Born To Lose"), Al Dexter ("Pistol Packin' Mama") and Floyd Tillman. Of them, only Tillman has had an LP reissue of his major performances.

His composition "Slipping Around" is widely regarded as the first big hit concerned with infidelity. His jazzy blue notes and slurred tones set the pattern for such artists as Willie Nelson. If Nelson's eccentric, expressive style fascinates you, just listen to the man who originated it.

- Hank Thompson

The Best of Hank Thompson *Capitol DT 1878*

Thompson straddles the fence between honky-tonk and western swing. His mixture of the two styles was hugely popular in the late 1940s and early 1950s; and he remains musically and professionally vital to this day.

This album contains the classic sounds of his "Wild Side of Life" (1950), "Whoa, Sailor" (1949), and "Humpty Dumpty Heart" (1948); but brings Thompson's consistent style up through "A Six Pack To Go" (1960) and "Hangover Tavern" (1961), illustrating the eternal verities of the honky-tonk style.

Chapter Nine

Southeastern Revival

Isaac Newton could have been discussing the music business when he wrote, "For every action there is an equal and opposite reaction." Despite the seemingly endless craving for innovation, there is a strong streak of tradition and revivalism in country music, and from time to time this atavistic urge surfaces.

Interestingly, it often surfaces in the guise of innovation—take the case of Hank Williams (who could have been discussed as easily in this section as in honky-tonk), who brought bright new songs to the world of country music when he burst on the scene in the late 1940s. His songs were new, and they were great, but they were also simple, as was his own sound; though his voice was unmistakable, there were echoes of Roy Acuff and Ernest Tubb, and his straightforward fiddle and steel guitar accompaniment was purely no-nonsense.

All this came in an era when silvery voiced singing cowboys, sweet strains of western swing, and mellow-voiced country singers like Red Foley were dominating country music. In fact, Hank Williams had trouble landing a record deal at first—he was too raw, too country, not slick enough. But it was precisely this no-frills country music sung by Williams, Kitty Wells, Webb Pierce, Carl Smith, and others that the public was ready to hear. It was so old it seemed new, and its greatest appeal was precisely in its lack of sophistication—the country music audience had had enough of that, and was ready for hard hitting gritty country music once more.

If there was a major change from years past, it was in the story these songs told. With the national success of Jimmy Wakely's "One Has

My Name, The Other Has My Heart," and "Slippin'
Around" (in 1948 and 1949 respectively) formerly
taboo subjects were now broached with a vengeance
by country singers and songwriters, and it became
these revivalist song stylists who by and large made
them work.

The southeastern sound is a term used for lack of a
better one. Singers from the western and western
swing genres tended to be pleasant baritones, with
laconic, sun-warmed, and often sophisticated vocal
stylings and phrasings. The singers covered in this
chapter tended to have higher-pitched voices, with
much of the soulful, close-mouthed feel of the Appala-
chians in their approach. It was clearly, identifiably
not western, nor western swing—it was *country*, by
God, and proud of it. In being so it laid the foundation
for much of what is heard today, and ironically for
another equal and opposite reaction: the ultra-slick
Nashville sound, to come a decade and a half later.

KITTY WELLS

Kitty Wells's voice is the near-perfect embodiment of
the southeastern sound: restrained, plaintive, high-
pitched, extremely moving in a repressed way. Yet,
interestingly, it was a central ingredient to her success
that while her sound was the embodiment of the high-
land singing tradition, her songs were often firm state-
ments by and for woman, and in addition she was the
first woman singer to tackle head-on the difficult problems of postwar America: alcoholism and infidelity,
drink and divorce; and all the while maintaining the
image of a simple, sweet, dignified, gingham-clad
country housewife.

She was born Muriel Deason in Nashville, Tennessee
in 1919, and married young Johnny Wright, who soon
founded what was to become a very popular duet,
Johnny and Jack, with Jack Anglin. The duet struggled
and gained ground throughout the late 1940s, and
occasionally Mrs. Wright, going under the stage name
of Kitty Wells (from the old folk song "Sweet Kitty
Wells") sang a song or two with the band. She obtained
her own record contract for RCA (Johnny and Jack's
label) in the late 1940s, but it was her first recording
for Decca, "It Wasn't God Who Made Honky-Tonk
Angels" (an answer to Hank Thompson's "Wild Side of
Life") in 1952 that brought her national success.

The song was pure Kitty Wells: doleful, filled with
repressed emotion, yet proud and a little bit sassy, too.
It was a woman's song, from a woman's point of view,
something the American woman was ready to hear,
and Kitty Wells became their spokeswoman.

THE LOUVIN BROTHERS

Ira (1924–1965) and Charlie (b. 1927) Loudermilk formed their mandolin-guitar duet act when the vogue for brother duets was ending in country music. Brother duets were exceptionally popular during the Depression, but by the late 1950s only The Everly Brothers, The Wilburn Brothers, and the Louvins remained as hitmakers.

The Louvin Brothers were the most mountain-sounding of these three teams. And if it had not been for the southeastern sound revival of the early 1950s they probably would have remained obscure. Indeed, they struggled for many many years before landing a spot on the Opry in 1955.

It is difficult to top the Louvins as pure expressions of southeastern soul. Charlie's full baritone voice richly complemented Ira's incredibly high, emotional tenor; and the two voices, effortlessly leaping in and out of harmony parts, were both strikingly complex and fervently sincere.

The Louvin Brothers were thought by the Opry management of the time to be a little dated, so today's listeners may have trouble getting used to their gospel-derived intensity, too. The brothers sing hard, with undisguised passion and feeling. Their backup instrumentation and recording sound is early Nashville at its fumbling best. But this pair still tells more about the spirit and meaning of pure country music than any book ever can.

MARTY ROBBINS

There is perhaps no one in the history of country music more difficult to categorize than Marty Robbins. The scope of his ability was vast. In his distinguished career Robbins performed western songs, rockabilly, honky-tonk, comedy, pop ballads, Hawaiian music, teenage material, Nashville Sound country songs, vaudeville, and blues. Since many of his earliest hits—"I'll Go On Alone," "I Couldn't Keep From Crying," "Singing the Blues"—had the emotional directness and open-throated qualities of southeastern singers, he has been placed in this chapter. He rose to stardom in 1953, when this revival was in full swing, but Robbins could easily fit in the Singing Cowboy, Nashville Sound, Singer/Songwriters, or Crossover chapters.

Marty Robbins was a true westerner, not a mountain man. A child of the Arizona desert, he was discovered in Phoenix by Little Jimmy Dickens in 1952 and brought to the attention of Columbia Records. A natural "heart" singer, Robbins scored his first top-ten country hit in 1953; and, with the exception of just three years, had a top-ten record every year until he died in late 1982.

In 1955 he recorded rockabilly music ("That's All Right"). In 1957 he recorded teen-themed material ("A White Sport Coat"). In 1959 his western songs made him an international celebrity ("El Paso"). In 1961 he pioneered the fuzz-tone guitar ("Don't Worry") that later became prominent in psychedelic rock music. In 1965 he took part in the folk boom (Gordon Lightfoot's "Ribbon of Darkness"). In the late 1960s he adopted Latin themes and rhythms. In the early 1970s he wrote highly successful pop music ballads ("You Gave Me a Mountain," "My Woman, My Woman, My Wife"). In 1976–77 he revived songs from the early years of the century ("Among My Souvenirs," "I Don't Know Why, I Just Do"). And he ended his career with the lushly arranged countrypolitan sound of the 1980s ("Some Memories Just Won't Die").

Marty Robbins (1925–1982) was the master of many styles. Through them all, however, he retained his nickname: "Old Golden Throat."

HANK SNOW

Hank Snow rose to prominence by reaching into the past, like most of the other southeastern revival acts. Unlike the mountain-influenced Louvins and Kitty Wells, however, Snow's revival was in song types, not vocal styles. He was tremendously in awe of Jimmie Rodgers and emulated him for years. He was fascinated by train songs and murder ballads. He resurrected sentimental old-time ballads and singing cowboy songs.

He molded all of these into a highly personal style, one of the most individual and distinctive in country history. Snow's instantly identifiable, back-of-the-palate tone and crisp diction have made him legendary. As an extremely deft flat-top acoustic guitar picker, Hank Snow's records have also been frequently marked by instrumental excellence as well.

Clarence Eugene "Hank" Snow was born in Nova Scotia in 1914. He got his first recording contract in 1936, and subsequently became the artist to have the longest continual career with one record label (RCA) in the history of show business.

He brought his remarkable nasal resonance to Nashville in 1950, the year of his giant hit "I'm Movin' On." From that time to the present his basic style has been relatively stable, although more modern instrumentation has done away with the once-prominent steel guitar licks of Kayton Roberts and his own tasty guitar stylings.

The 1979 Hall of Fame inductee still entertains each week on The Grand Ole Opry.

SELECTED RECORDINGS

- Kitty Wells

The Kitty Wells Story *MCA 2-4031*

- Kitty Wells

The Golden Years *Rounder SS-13*

Miss Kitty has a wonderful, unmistakable, piercing, high, keening delivery that brings out the "country" in country songs. "It Wasn't God Who Made Honky Tonk Angels" started it all. But there are many more fine songs on the MCA set that became equally big hits for her and at the same time paved the way for acceptance of solo female singers in country music.

The problem, as with all the MCA reissues, is that the original simple country instrumentation of those early hits has been replaced by "modern" instrumentation. This defect is not the case with the Rounder reissue, which features all the original bounced fiddle bows, steel guitar wails, and throbbing rhythm guitars. It has few of Wells's biggest hits, but more thoroughly demonstrates how this woman became The Queen of Country Music.

Kitty is at once intensely emotional and incredibly reserved as a performer. It is this dichotomy that makes her such an involving, moving vocalist.

- The Louvin Brothers

The Louvin Brothers *Rounder 07*

If you're already a country fan, but haven't yet heard The Louvin Brothers, you are in for a treat. Once you've heard these fellows sing, you'll understand how Emmylou Harris became a Louvin addict. If you're unfamiliar with their songwriting, you'll understand why she recorded "If I Could Only Win Your Love," "When I Stop Dreaming," and "You're Learning."

The Louvins were arguably the best country brother duet of all, for hardly any others have matched their combination of expert songwriting and goosebump harmony singing. Imagine The Everly Brothers more country, a bit harsher, somewhat higher-voiced, and a lot less teenaged, and you'll have an idea of the Louvin style.

As with several of country music's authentic geniuses, *any* Louvin Brothers record is a good one to get. In addition to the Rounder Records reissues, Capitol has put out the old Louvin gospel efforts again.

- Marty Robbins

Marty's Greatest Hits *Columbia CL 1325*

- Marty Robbins

More Greatest Hits *Columbia CS 8435*
- Marty Robbins

Greatest Hits Vol. III *Columbia C 30571*

These three LPs define the scope of Marty's art prior to 1970. The first, including as it does straight-ahead country ("Singing the Blues"), western material ("The Hanging Tree"), rockabilly ("Long Tall Sally") and teen pop material ("A White Sport Coat"), is the most delightful. It is also quintessentially 1950s, since its scope is 1955–1959.

More Greatest Hits focuses mainly on the western material of the "El Paso" era. The third LP's scope is 1962–1970 with an emphasis on songs from the late 1960s. Curiously, there is no Marty Robbins collection that reissues such classic Nashville Sound smashes from the early 1960s as "Begging To You," "Ruby Ann," "Count Me Out," and "Cigarettes & Coffee Blues."

In the 1980s Columbia released two more compilations, *Encore* and *Biggest Hits,* but these are incompetently programmed and ignorantly put together, as might usually be expected from modern executives.

- Hank Snow

The Best of Hank Snow *RCA LSP-3478*

Like Robbins, Snow is capable of a wide range of styles. He was a leader, along with Johnny & Jack, in the little-documented country rhumba craze of the early 1950s, as this set's "Rhumba Boogie" bears witness. His flare for ballads is illustrated by "Let Me Go, Lover" and "I Don't Hurt Anymore." This, the first volume of RCA's packages of Snow's biggest hits, contains mainly early 1950s material, but a few 1960s titles like the famous tongue-twister "I've Been Everywhere" and the saga song "Miller's Cave" are also included.

Hank's north-of-the-border nasality, distinctive accent, and frequent wide-open-spaces song subject matter clearly mark him as the Nova Scotia individualist he is. His clipped enunciation of a word followed by a long drawl on the next makes listening to him always intriguing. Newcomers to his odd style may find Snow off-putting at first, but be forewarned that increased listening to this fellow is addictive. And he is one of the most-recorded artists in country music history.

OTHER RECOMMENDED RECORDINGS OF 1950s COUNTRY:
- Various Artists

Country Hits of the 1940s *Capitol SM 884*

- Various Artists

Country Hits of the 1950s *Capitol SM 885*

Capitol Records was organized in the 1940s and by mid-decade was scoring country hits consistently. The young company signed up many of the new honky-tonk stylists, gave West Coast talent an outlet, discovered several fine instrumentalists, and emphasized some Texas and Oklahoma talents that Nashville missed.

The first record collects some hits that brought the young Los Angeles company to prominence, including Margaret Whiting and Jimmy Wakely's "Slipping Around," Leon Payne's "I Love You Because," and Jack Guthrie's "Oklahoma Hills." These give an insight and feel for the late 1940s and early 1950s in country music. The set's major flaw is that several of the hits ("Smoke Smoke Smoke That Cigarette," "Pistol Packin' Mama") are later re-recordings and not the originals.

The second set is another fine introduction to the era. Several of its hits are by artists who have been overlooked in the history books. "Don't Let the Stars Get In Your Eyes" made Skeets McDonald a star. "You Better Not Do That" by Tommy Collins was one of the top-ten records of 1954. And long before Faron Young was crooning "It's Four In the Morning" he was delivering uptempo delights like "If You Ain't Lovin' (Then You Ain't Livin')."

- Cowboy Copas

Best of Cowboy Copas *Starday SLP-958*

Before he died in the same plane crash that killed Patsy Cline and Hawkshaw Hawkins in 1963, Lloyd "Cowboy" Copas accumulated an impressive string of hits. All of these were archetypical tunes of the times. His popularity was at a peak with "Alabam," "Filipino Baby," "Signed, Sealed and Delivered," and "Tragic Romance," among the others included on this reissue.

- Moon Mullican

Greatest Hits *Starday 398*

They call Moon Mullican the greatest hillbilly piano player who ever lived. That's probably because he fused rockabilly, honky-tonk, western swing, boogie-woogie, Cajun, and old-time religion. During his creative peak in the late 1940s and early 1950s, "Cherokee Boogie," "Jole Blon," "Sweeter Than the Flowers," and "I'll Sail My Ship Alone" demonstrated his incredible versatility.

- The Maddox Brothers and Rose

The Maddox Brothers and Rose, 1946–1951, Vol. 1 *Arhoolie 5016*

The Maddox family comprised another important fusion group of the late 1940s and early 1950s. They're cited equally by rockabilly, honky-tonk, and southeastern revival devotees as pure exponents. As a band, this group illustrates country music at the point of its transitions between innocence and cold modern reality, between rural and urban experience, and between small-time show biz to big-time entertainment.

Chapter Ten
Rockabilly

Rockabilly music was born in the South in the years after World War II. Its traditional birthplace is usually given as Memphis, since many of the form's most important performers were on that city's Sun Records label from 1954 to 1960, rockabilly's formative years. But rockabilly music also flourished in California, Texas, and the Southwest.

Stylistically, rockabilly music is an amalgam of country, swing, black rhythm & blues, and gospel. Lyrically, it was about teenagers; visually, it featured rebellious, longhaired young men with electric guitars.

Musically, rockabilly was a small combo sound. Instrumentation varied widely, but generally the electric lead guitar, acoustic rhythm guitar, drums, and either stand-up or electric bass were the core of a rockabilly band. Piano and/or saxophone were also sometimes present. The instruments were lightly amplified. As rockabilly matured little echo chamber effects became common in the music. The rhythm was highly syncopated, with little "bottom" in the beat; and short instrumental licks and breaks were taken by the players, rather than fullfledged solos.

The vocal style was taken from country music. The "teardrop" honky-tonk singing style was modified by rockabilly singers, who frequently added short "cries" or hiccoughing effects to the country vocal repertoire.

The rockabilly sound and style were drawn from equal parts of black and white Southern culture. Working-class white youths married country's emotional directness with a black beat and came up with music that symbolized teenage rebellion in the 1950s. The visceral singing style, aggressive stage mannerisms, and rhythmic intensity of rockabilly music made it the most popular country music genre of its era; and its appeal has continued for 25 years since, as witnessed by the numerous rockabilly revival acts who have appeared since the rockabilly era "ended."

The sound of the slapped stand-up bass, boogie-woogie piano, and staccato electric guitar that characterized classic rockabilly music have now been absorbed into mainstream country music. But when rockabilly began, it created a musical revolution. From it grew the most popular music of all time, rock & roll.

ELVIS PRESLEY

They called him "The Hillbilly Cat" when he started performing in Memphis, Louisiana, Texas, and Arkansas in 1954. Although Bill Haley predated him as a country singer who adopted the black beat, Presley is the man who ignited the rockabilly fire.

Elvis Presley transformed rockabilly into rock'n'roll at Sun Records.

He was a country boy who dressed in the flashy clothes of ghetto blacks. He was a devout Southern Baptist who seethed with sex, ground his hips, and growled his vocals. He was a softspoken, polite young man who dressed like a hoodlum, greased his hair, and curled his lips in a snarl. In the character of Elvis Presley were all the contradictions of postwar Southern youths. He was rural meeting urban, simple sentiment meeting ferocious emotion, white meeting black, child meeting adult. He electrified America. He became the most popular entertainer in the world.

Elvis's later career as a ballad singer and mainstream rock & roller has somewhat obscured his rockabilly roots. But his earliest recordings are textbook examples of the form. On them, you can clearly hear his debt to country music, as well as his influences from pop, gospel, and black music of the day.

His childhood was spent in a shack in Tupelo, Mississippi. His teenage years were spent in a Memphis housing project. His adulthood was spent in a white-columned Southern mansion. Elvis Presley (1935–1977) lived a country boy's fantasy. He rose from humble hillbilly origins and parlayed his native musical ability into worldwide acclaim.

CARL PERKINS

Of the major rockabilly figures, Carl Perkins is at once the most "country" in overall sound and the most innovative as an electric instrumentalist. Although he has never lost his country music following, Perkins is claimed as a rock pioneer as well.

Born in Lake City, Tennessee in 1932, he initially signed with Memphis's Sun Records as a country artist. His bluesy vocal style and sizzling guitar playing were naturals for the emerging youth market, however, and when his "Blue Suede Shoes" was released in 1956 it was a smash success on both country and pop music charts.

A nearly fatal auto accident prevented Perkins from cashing in on that record's success; so Presley quickly overtook him as the rockabilly star in the national spotlight. And although Perkins released an excellent string of teen-themed follow-up singles, he never regained his initial momentum.

Still an exciting rockabilly artist, Carl Perkins continues to tour Europe and America regularly. A long stint with the Johnny Cash roadshow in the 1960s cemented his reputation as a songwriter ("Daddy Sang Bass," "Honey Don't") and live performer with contemporary country fans. Now he tours on his own with his sons playing bass and drums, a living testament to the enduring power of rockabilly music.

JERRY LEE LEWIS

Lewis, born in Ferriday, Louisiana in 1935, could be one of the few true musical geniuses of contemporary country music. Although his records are consistently fascinating and he always sells well, his reputation is built upon his mesmerizing intensity as a live performer. He needs nothing more than a piano and an audience to put on "the greatest live show on earth," as it has often been called.

With his fingers pounding the keyboard, his roaring baritone blasting into a microphone, his head twitching in musical ecstasy, and his feet stomping in rhythm, Jerry Lee Lewis is the embodiment of the crazed rockabilly man. Perhaps not surprisingly, he is also capable of almost frightening vulnerability and sensitivity when he turns his hand to straight country music.

Jerry Lee is a master at the keyboard. With seeming unconcern for proper time and place he fills the spaces in his songs with shimmering runs and dazzling obbligatos. His fusion of boogie-woogie, honky-tonk, and ragtime elements makes him one of the most creative piano players in country music history.

His skill in a wide range of musical styles also makes him one of the most difficult artists to categorize in country music. He fits easily into the classic definition of rock & roll, since he exhibits a close kinship with men like Little Richard and Chuck Berry; but his unmistakably country qualities lead to his inevitable inclusion on lists of rockabilly pioneers, despite the fact that his music bears little relationship to that of Buddy Holly, Carl Perkins, The Everly Brothers, or Eddie Cochran.

Jerry Lee Lewis is, in sum, an American original.

JOHNNY CASH

With his boom-chicka-boom bass line and steady, walking beat Johnny Cash was rockabilly music's minimalist. Of all his compatriots at Sun Records, he stayed closest to his country roots. He subsequently enjoyed the greatest success as a straight country performer.

As a result, Cash was the performer who brought rockabilly into the country music mainstream. Throughout his long career he has always featured rockabilly numbers alongside his country ballads, historical saga songs, and gospel numbers.

The Man In Black, as he is known, had a typical country background. Born to tenant farmers in Arkansas in 1932, Cash's first serious attempts at music were while he was in Germany in the Air Force. Upon his return he took his original songs to the little creative hotbed at Sun and scored immediate hits with "Hey Porter," "Folsom Prison Blues," and "I Walk the Line." All three are claimed by rockabilly enthusiasts as well as country fans.

In 1958 he made the transition to Nashville stardom on the much larger Columbia Records, where he has remained. Cash recorded an excellent string of country concept LPs in the 1960s and 1970s, achieved national television stardom, then revived his rockabilly roots in the 1980s.

He is now virtually synonymous with Nashville commercial country music and has reached the status of an elder statesman. But among his many accomplishments are some superb rockabilly gems.

THE EVERLY BROTHERS

Don (b. 1937) and Phil (b. 1939) Everly were the sons of Kentucky country musicians who had been on radio since the time they were children. When they came to Nashville in the 1950s, they brought country brother-duet harmonies to the teenage music of the day.

The Everlys' music was considerably sweeter and more pop oriented than the rockabilly produced in Memphis or on the West Coast. It lacked raw edges and was more cautiously produced than most rockabilly, but it had enough drive and rhythm to make it immensely popular with teenagers.

The pair's 1950s material on Cadence Records featured the electric guitar work of Chet Atkins and a direct, open sound. The 1960s material, on Warner Brothers, was considerably slicker but still contained rockabilly traces. The 1970s saw the Everlys attempt a return to their country roots until they broke up in 1973. Don has continued to record and perform a synthesis of country and rock. Phil's solo work has been more in a pop or easy-listening vein.

BUDDY HOLLY

Although Buddy Holly never had a country hit, recent reevaluations of his music have placed him more and more in the country camp as a rockabilly innovator. Charles Hardin Holley (the e in his last name was dropped only after he signed his first record contract) was born September 7, 1936, in Lubbock, Texas, and grew up listening to Hank Williams and the Mexican-flavored country music (called Tex-Mex) of that area.

His first band billed itself as offering "Western and Bop" music, indicating Holly's basic approach. He tried recording in Nashville as a straight country artist, but soon repaired to Clovis, New Mexico where he could better work on his personal musical vision.

Holly's startling songwriting, hot band, pure rockabilly vocals, and dance beat soon resulted in a solid string of teen hits. These ended prematurely when he was killed in a plane crash in 1959.

BILL HALEY

The leader of a series of good local country bands in the late 1940s and early 1950s, Bill Haley (1925–1981) became the unlikely launcher of rock & roll when his 1954–55 fusion of "jump" blues music and country took off like a rocket. Songs like "Rock Around the Clock," "See You Later, Alligator," and "Shake, Rattle, & Roll" turned him into an international rock & roll star overnight.

Haley had bands like The Down Homers, The Four Aces of Western Swing, and The Saddle Pals before he formed his famous Comets. The last named group brought elements of boogie-woogie, swing music, rhythm & blues, and country together and in so doing became rockabilly's first headline attraction.

SELECTED RECORDINGS

● Elvis Presley

The Sun Sessions *RCA AFM 1-1675*

Presley's later work as a Las Vegas crooner, mainstream rock singer, and country/pop ballad moaner has obscured the raw intensity and fire of his first recordings. Those early Sun Records singles, however, are what brought him fame; and they remain powerful musical experiences.

The King's sizzling, hot, howling, growling work on these early singles was nearly forgotten until RCA reissued them in 1976. What had also been overlooked in the 20 or so years that elapsed between Elvis's first recordings and their reappearance was the eclectic nature of his repertoire. Like all of country's great innovators, Elvis fused a variety of styles.

"Milkcow Blues Boogie," "Good Rockin' Tonight," "That's All Right," "Mystery Train," and "Baby Let's Play House" came from black tradition. "Blue Moon of Kentucky," "I Love You Because," "I'll Never Let You Go," and "Just Because" were pure country in origin. "I Don't Care If the Sun Don't Shine" and "Blue Moon" were Tin Pan Alley tunes. And the rest of Elvis's early songs were written by his fellow Sun pioneers.

Presley took this disparate hodgepodge of tunes and forged something new and fresh and different. Even today, what he did is a revelation to hear.

● Carl Perkins

Original Golden Hits *Sun 111*

Rock fans mainly know Carl Perkins songs like "Honey Don't" and "Match Box" from The Beatles' versions. "Boppin' the Blues," "Everybody's Trying

To Be My Baby" and "Dixie Fried" are likewise well-known from later rock bands' renditions. Even "Blue Suede Shoes" is better known from Elvis Presley's recording than from Perkins's own.

This LP demonstrates why Carl Perkins has retained his reputation despite all that. It contains all you need to know about classic rockabilly songwriting, singing, and guitar playing. In England, especially, the man is still regarded as a guitar hero, and there is a boxed set of his complete Sun recordings available.

- Jerry Lee Lewis

Original Golden Hits—Volume 1 *Sun 102*
- Jerry Lee Lewis

The Best of Jerry Lee Lewis
Smash (Mercury) SRS-67131

There is no such thing as an uninteresting Jerry Lee Lewis record; and those interested in the full chronicle of his magnificent output will want to pick up the other two volumes of his Sun material, *The Best Of Vol. 2* collection of his Mercury hits, and *The Best Of* compilation on Elektra of his recent country and rockabilly efforts.

The Sun LP contains his first single, the fascinatingly self-confident "Crazy Arms." Like it, Lewis's version of "You Win Again" (also included) reveals his total command of classic country. Alongside them, however, are the fire-breathing "Great Balls of Fire," "Whole Lotta Shakin' Going On," and "Breathless," the trio of tunes that guaranteed him immortality.

The Mercury/Smash album presents Jerry Lee as a master honky-tonk stylist. "What's Made Milwaukee Famous" (1968), "She Even Woke Me Up To Say Goodbye" (1969), and "Another Place, Another Time" (1968) marked his reemergence in country music. These and their companions on this collection reveal the country soul behind the rockin' wild man who has been a headliner for 25 years.

- Johnny Cash

Original Golden Hits Vol. 1 *Sun 100*
- Johnny Cash

Greatest Hits Vol. 1 *Columbia CS 9478*
- Johnny Cash

Encore *Columbia FC 37355*

With his incredibly craggy features and rumbling monotonic voice, Johnny Cash has done more with less than perhaps anyone else in popular music. His secret is believability. Whether he's vocally swaggering to a rockabilly beat, as on the Sun LP; roaring country ballads and story songs, as on the

Columbia collection of his mid-1960s hits; or essaying the songs of country music's finest young writers, as on the *Encore* LP; he remains a completely convincing interpreter.

His output has been prodigious. Besides these three hits collections from the 1950s, 1960s, and 1970s, there are many fine concept albums. Among the best are *Bitter Tears, Ballads of the True West,* and *Blood Sweat and Tears* (all on Columbia).

And some of his finest LPs have been in recent years. *Gone Girl, Silver, Rockabilly Blues,* and *The Adventures of Johnny Cash* have demonstrated that his remarkable powers are undimmed by time. All are on Columbia. For the smaller Cachet, he recorded the excellent *A Believer Sings the Truth* gospel LP just prior to his 1980 election into the Country Music Hall of Fame.

● **The Everly Brothers**
Golden Hits of the Everly Brothers
Warner Brothers 1471
The Everlys are quintessential country soul, perfect harmony vocalists, and masters of boppin' rhythms. Their 1950s rockabilly performances have never been equalled by others.

Unfortunately, those Cadence Records singles ("Bye Bye Love," "Wake Up Little Susie," "When Will I Be Loved," "Bird Dog," "All I Have To Do Is Dream") are as of this writing unavailable. They have been packaged and repackaged on labels like Barnaby, Janus, Pickwick, K-Tel, and dozens of smaller ones. There's no single LP title to be cited here; just find those records on any label you can.

Do not, however, look for those classic Everly titles on Warner Brothers. There is a Warner collection that features them, but do not be fooled. That album contains 1960s re-recordings of rockabilly Everly Brothers, not the original tracks.

One Warners album that *does* contain hits the brothers did in their original form is this one. Although songs like "Cathy's Clown," "Walk Right Back," "Crying In The Rain," and "Ebony Eyes" aren't nearly as purely rockabilly as the Everlys' early material, they're great records nonetheless.

● **Buddy Holly**
A Rock & Roll Collection *MCA 2-4009 (two-record set)*
This two-disc set is the single best introduction to the music of Buddy Holly and his Crickets. The lilting, melodic numbers "Maybe Baby" and "It Doesn't Matter Anymore" contrast with the hic-coughing teen-beat tunes "Peggy Sue," "Rave On," and "That'll Be the Day" to demonstrate the range of

Holly's ability. "Heartbeat," "Love's Made a Fool of You," and "Crying, Waiting, Hoping," indicate that he might have developed into a full-fledged pop composer. But "Oh Boy!" and "Not Fade Away" show that he had a rockabilly heart.

● **Bill Haley & The Comets**
Golden Hits *MCA 2-4010 (two-record set)*
This double-LP documents the first tentative steps country music took toward rockabilly. As such, it is certainly worth having. Beyond that, though, it is a souvenir of some of the niftiest little ol' toe-tappers of the 1950s. It's hard to imagine that the light syncopation of "Rock Around the Clock" drove teenagers into frenzies, but it did. This, after all, was the birth of the rockabilly beat.

OTHER RECOMMENDED ROCKABILLY RECORDINGS

● **Eddie Cochran**
Legendary Masters
United Artists UA UAR-LWB-9959
Eddie Cochran is the outstanding example of West Coast rockabilly. Along with Gene Vincent and Wanda Jackson, he is the most imitated of the second-string rockabillies. Cochran's hot guitar playing, excellent songwriting, and piledriving beat make him one of the most exciting performers of the rockabilly era. His music still sizzles so strongly that "Summertime Blues" and several of his other masterpieces have never grown old.

● **Johnny Burnette**
Tear It Up *Solid Smoke 8001*
Perhaps more than any other currently available LP, this Solid Smoke reissue of Johnny Burnette's early music captures the true spirit of rockabilly music. It is wonderfully simple stuff, full of high spirits, enthusiasm, bounce, and crazy, crazy rhythm. Burnette and his boys sound like nothing so much as a bunch of hopped-up hillbillies having the time of their lives with joyous teenage dance music.

Chapter Eleven

The Nashville Sound

The coming of rock ultimately created a large hole in the fabric of American music: the pop music it had replaced sounded stale and dated, while the country music of the early 1950s was simply too regional to attain widespread national success. As for rock itself, it was the music of the youth of the era, leaving many cold, and filling more than a few with intense dislike.

There was a large segment of the music buying market—larger, probably, than anyone dreamed—who, if they were not actively looking, were certainly willing to accept a musical style which did not contain the implicit threat or sexuality of rock, the impenetrable hipness of jazz, the casual insincerity of old-line pop, or the mawkishness and regionalism of honky-tonk and country music. This large market was tapped with astonishing skill by a handful of executives and producers in Nashville; these men, with a smaller handful of pleasant singers with "crossover" potential and musicians of consummate skill, forged a gentle, mellow, easy-listening brand of country music which, partly through aggressive self-promotion, became known as the Nashville Sound.

Despite myriad musical changes, and the emergence of dozens of new entertainers; despite movements, shifts in audience demographics and automation, it remains, 20 years and more later, the dominant force in country music heard on the radio. New artists, new variations of sounds come and go, but this middle-of-the-road sound, designed for widest appeal, is still the basis for the vast majority of country recordings.

Traditionalists may bemoan its creation and its dominance, but there are two things to remember: it filled a very definite need, and it was, at the time, a matter of survival. The musical style created by Chet Atkins and a handful of other musicians and producers pulled Nashville up by its bootstraps at a time when it was reeling from the effects of rock on bookings, record sales, and popularity.

And what is the Nashville Sound? It is easier to describe its origins and its place in music history than its actual sound, for it is actually rather vague. Guitar-oriented (particularly in the rhythm), it nonetheless freely used background voices and string sections to "sweeten" the sound, usage virtually unheard of in country music before that time. It is a subtle, unobtrusive feel—no ringing banjos or shivering steel guitars here—which let the lyrics and the smooth voice of the singer tell the story. It is laid back, certainly—too laid back for some—but that is its niche; and though it is no longer called the Nashville Sound, it continues to fill that niche as adult-oriented country music, more popular today than ever before.

CHET ATKINS

The Nashville Sound was the creation of basically four influential Music City studio personalities. One was arranger and background vocalist Anita Kerr. Another was pianist/bandleader Owen Bradley. Columbia executive Don Law, once a member of the London Choral Society, was the third. The fourth was guitarist Chet Atkins.

Born in Luttrell, Tennessee in 1924, Atkins had the most solidly country background of the quartet, but he was also deeply influenced by pop and jazz music. He began his musical career in middle Tennessee as a hillbilly fiddler and guitarist. He came to Nashville, in fact, as a musician for The Carter Family.

Large amounts of session work in the rapidly growing studios of Nashville sharpened his guitar-playing skills; and he quickly mastered a wide variety of picking styles. Although essentially self-taught, Atkins became adept at jazz, flamenco, rockabilly, and classical stylings as well as flat-top country picking.

His faultless execution and quick-study abilities soon made him indispensible in recording sessions. By the mid-1950s he was leading them and assuming the mantle of a Nashville Sound record producer.

Like fellow producers Law and Bradley, Atkins favored high, open-tuned rhythm guitars played over a lightly-brushed beat. Over this foundation were laid violins (not fiddles) and soft, soothing background

Chet Atkins and his guitar were instrumental in creating the Nashville Sound.

voices (usually either The Anita Kerr Singers or The Jordanaires). The lead vocalist rode on top of all this, singing country lyrics with heart but not histrionics.

EDDY ARNOLD

Once billed as the Tennessee Plowboy, Eddy Arnold was one of the first Nashville singers to radically change his image in reaching for the vast, untapped market left open by the advent of rock. Possessor of a clear tenor voice of great range and feel, Eddy—who was born near Henderson, Tennessee, in 1918—got his first national exposure as a member of Pee Wee King's Golden West Cowboys from 1942–1945. He joined the Grand Ole Opry shortly thereafter, and his first hit records followed: "It's a Sin" and "I'll Hold You In My Heart" in 1947, "Bouquet of Roses," "Anytime," "Just a Little Lovin' " in 1948, and many more in following years.

Gradually his voice deepened into a soothing baritone, and he shed the Tennessee plowboy image with the big grin to that of a well dressed—often tuxedo-clad—entertainer, relaxed in a wide variety of situations, most of them far removed from the tentshow circuit and small town high school auditorium. In this new guise, armed with his powerful charm and warm voice, he became one of the first country artists to have his own television show, and continued a long string of middle-of-the-road hit records such as "What's He

Doing In My World," "Make The World Go Away," "I Want To Go With You," and "Then You Can Tell Me Goodbye."

A success in both country music and adult popular, Eddy Arnold is estimated to have sold something like 50 to 60 million records, a figure approached by very few others. He currently lives in genial semiretirement in Brentwood, a Nashville suburb.

JIM REEVES

Few singers epitomize growth and development as does Jim Reeves (1924–1964), the Texas-born singer with the smooth velvet voice. Though his early love was baseball, an injury turned his attention to a second career, that of announcer and singer, where he worked at a number of stations before joining the Louisiana Hayride as a staff announcer.

His recording career bloomed with the release of the hit single "Mexican Joe" in 1953; quickly signed to RCA, he began a long string of hits in a straightforward country style, including "Bimbo," "Yonder Comes a Sucker," "According To My Heart," and "Am I Losing You." His recording of "Four Walls" marked a turning point, however, for with this record he turned from the path of deep country music—it was rather clearly labeled dead end by this time (1957)—and helped define the "Nashville Sound" with his smooth, across-the-board approach, the use of gentle voices and strings, and relaxed, soothing feel.

A singer of great technique and versatility, Jim Reeves had the ability to carry this off, and after several others hits—"Anna Marie," "Blue Boy," and "Billy Bayou"—he struck again with the biggest song of his career in 1959: "He'll Have To Go," one of those great records that still sounds as fresh today as when it was new.

PATSY CLINE

Like Jim Reeves, Patsy Cline (1932–1963) had the ability to keep the "heart" in her voice while blending with The Nashville Sound's cool, elegant orchestral settings. This quality made her the leading contender for Kitty Wells's throne as Queen of Country Music in the late 1950s and early 1960s.

Patsy's real name was Virginia Patterson Hensley. A native of Winchester, Virginia, she initially performed as a straight country singer, capable of yodelling or any of the other country vocal techniques. After her arrival in Nashville, producer Owen Bradley brought out the pop qualities in her delivery. He also brought her the cream of the crop of songs that Nashville songwriters had to offer. A star was born.

Cline's career was cut short by an airplane crash March 5, 1963, but like Jim Reeves and Elvis Presley, her records have continued to sell steadily since her death. She was made a posthumous member of the Country Music Hall of Fame in 1973.

SELECTED RECORDINGS

- Chet Atkins

Legendary Performer Vol. 1 *RCA CPL-1-2503*

During his long career as the most recorded solo instrumentalist in popular music, Chet Atkins has never made an LP that is consistently satisfying. To hear him at his best, isolated tracks from albums spanning the past 25 years must be gleaned. If these are ever put together, a portrait of an extraordinarily proficient instrumentalist will emerge.

An attempt to do that has been made on this album, more than on any of the other *Best Of* and *Greatest Hits* RCA packages. Atkins's absorption of the staccato, early electric stylings of Les Paul is evident, as is his fascination with the echoey, plasticene sound that bubbles along like soap suds on water. Chet is a cool, technically dazzling stylist who is committed to wide popular acceptance. Thus, the strings and pop music arrangements that dominate all Nashville Sound albums are present here as well.

- Eddy Arnold

The Best of Eddy Arnold *RCA AYL-1-3675*

On the strength of his honey vocals on the songs collected on this LP, Eddy Arnold became the most successful and wealthy crooner in Nashville history. He's sort of an outdoor, folksy version of Perry Como. In Eddy Arnold's vocals, country hearts break a little more gently, the world is a little less bitter and lonely, and truths are delivered with the reassuring directness of a country preacher.

Arnold is an effective balladeer because of his soft-spoken sentimentality. There are no real tears here and no rough edges. Eddy Arnold is as smooth as molasses in July. And somehow, even with the strings and voices, he remains just that "country."

- Jim Reeves

The Best of Jim Reeves *RCA AYL-1-3678*

In spite of Eddy Arnold's undeniably wider popularity, Jim Reeves gets the nod as the ultimate male Nashville Sound singer. His velvet voice was complemented by Atkins's lush orchestrations like no other singer's. The marriage of country and pop music was consummated by Reeves's ability to be warm and expressive, yet controlled and distant.

He was effortlessly affecting. What seems on the surface to be merely pleasant, becomes deeply moving on repeated listenings. The feelings in these songs are complex, although the lyrics are simple. Somehow, Jim Reeves brought both qualities out. Once you've heard one, you'll crave more.

● Patsy Cline

The Patsy Cline Story *MCA 2-4038*

Cline retained a country "teardrop" in her delivery in spite of producer Owen Bradley's orchestral settings. Bradley was a much less gimmicky producer than Atkins. His Nashville Sound records are consequently rather more restrained.

Patsy Cline was his ultimate country success. For him, she played down her country characteristics. For her, he played down his popular music background. The results were records full of tension and dynamics. And that is probably why Cline's reputation as a singer continues to grow year after year. "I Fall To Pieces," "Walking After Midnight," "Crazy," "She's Got You," and "Sweet Dreams" have never grown old.

This voice is full of heart, love, and pain.

OTHER RECOMMENDED NASHVILLE SOUND RECORDINGS

● The Browns

Best of the Browns *RCA ANL-1-1083*

The Nashville Sound went down in country music history because it attracted the vast pop music audience to the delights of country music. Eddy Arnold, Jim Reeves, and Patsy Cline all achieved big pop music hits by singing the ditties of Nashville tunesmiths backed by voices and strings and rhythm guitars. The soft loveliness of the three Brown siblings, Jim Ed, Maxine, and Bonnie, also graced the pop charts. Their perfect tones on "The Three Bells (Little Jimmy Brown)" and other hits are nice discoveries for a novice.

● Bobby Bare

This Is Bobby Bare *RCA VPS-6090*

Although not as strong a singer as the other Nashville Sound vocalists, Bobby Bare made a significant contribution to the style because of his unerring good taste in songs. Some of Music Row's timeless tunes are collected here. "Detroit City," "500 Miles Away From Home," and "The Streets of Baltimore" are just three among them.

- Johnny Horton
Greatest Hits *Columbia CS-8396*
Columbia's biggest pop hits from the country field
came with saga songs. These were folk-styled com-
positions that told a tale, accompanied by all the
best production tricks the Nashville musicians
could muster. Some memorables were Jimmy Dean's
"Big Bad John," Stonewall Jackson's "Waterloo,"
Lefty Frizzell's "Long Black Veil," Marty Robbins's
"El Paso," and several of Johnny Horton's hits.

Horton possessed one of the most electrifying
voices of his era. He scored massive hits with "North
To Alaska," "Sink the Bismark," and "The Battle of
New Orleans," but even some of his lesser known
numbers on this LP ("Whispering Pines," "All for the
Love of a Girl") are impressive. Johnny Horton
(1929–1960) has never achieved the recognition of
some of the other Nashville Sound artists, but his
reputation grows still and his records still sell.

- Brenda Lee
The Brenda Lee Story *MCA 2-4012*
- Roy Orbison
The All-Time Greatest Hits
Monument KWG2784-38384-1
- Bobby Goldsboro
10th Anniversary Album *United Artists LWB-311*
The ultimate measure of the success of the Nashville
Sound artists and producers was that they were able
to place Southern or country vocalists directly onto
the pop music charts, bypassing the country music
audience completely. During the 1960s, Music City
songwriters and singers proved conclusively that
Nashville could be a profitable pop music center by
taking the Nashville Sound developed in country
music to further lengths.

Pop music had been a part of the Nashville music
scene for years. In fact, the first million-seller produced by Nashville was "Near You" (1947) by the
Francis Craig Orchestra.

A decade later, diminutive Brenda Lee began her
astounding string of hits. Her big-voiced ballads
paved the way for Roy Orbison's semioperatic productions; and her bluesy, soulful numbers also pre-
figured Orbison's success with rock and soul. Still
later, Bobby Goldsboro became a third Southern
vocalist to win wide pop acceptance from a Nashville base.

All three of these artists demonstrated the univer-
sality of the "soul" in country singers. All three also
subsequently became major country stars.

Chapter Twelve

Bakersfield

There is not a Bakersfield "sound" as such, in the sense of a Nashville Sound, but there was for over a decade one of the most forceful country music movements in the recent past emanating from that hot, dry little city up in California's San Joaquin Valley.

It was a combination of two movements, really: it was the continuation of the honky-tonk tradition, which had always been stronger in the West than in the East, with the infusion of some talented new blood. And it was the perfect antidote to the pervasive blandness of the Nashville Sound's more tired efforts, for the music from Bakersfield was warm (rather than cool), and heavy on steel guitars and fiddles, with a touch of the rockabilly's Telecaster guitars thrown in for good measure. It was music for people who felt country music was slipping away, and it might have remained a small conservative stand had it not been for the outstanding talents of the members of the movement: Merle Haggard, Buck Owens, Wynn Stewart, and others.

That a California based movement should be based in Bakersfield is due to but one thing: that's where Buck Owens is from, and his great success and sharp concern for business allowed him to build a mini-empire there. Perhaps more significant than Owens's success at the time, or the success of the movement for a decade or more, is that it was precisely during the middle and late 1960s that a lot of young musicians (ex-folkies, rockers, or both) became interested in country music, and it was not the Nashville Sound which inspired them. It was the subtly sung folk poetry of Merle Haggard, the strident harmony and red-hot picking of Buck Owens's

Buckaroos, and much of the country music which has emanated from everywhere but Nashville has owed a debt to the Bakersfield movement of the 1960s.

The movement today is no longer a movement; its members are now individual artists who continue their successful careers, having once been a part of a loose confederacy. Supplanted by Austin for creative energy in the early 1970s, Bakersfield remains Buck Owens's base, but has returned to being the hot little California city it once was, no longer threatening Nashville for dominance in the music field.

BUCK OWENS

Born in Sherman, Texas in 1929, and raised in Arizona, Alvis Edgar Owens moved to Bakersfield, California in 1951, and quickly established himself as a local guitarist of some reknown; he did not begin serious singing until much later.

Buck was signed to Capitol Records in 1957, and had his first hit in 1959: "Under Your Spell Again." Heavy on steel and fiddle, with the jumpy tenor vocals that marked his records for years, it was sung in a tender, subdued, but pure country style. This was followed by a long string of hit records: "Above and Beyond," "Excuse Me" (1960), "Fooling Around" and "Under the Influence of Love" (1961), "Act Naturally" (1963), "My Heart Skips a Beat" (1964), "Tiger By The Tail" and "Buckaroo" (1965), "Waiting' In the Welfare Line" (1966), "Sam's Place" (1967), and "Tall Dark Stranger" (1969).

Buck enjoyed these years as one of the top stars in country music, and built a music and business complex in Bakersfield. After this time, however, he seemed to grope for the magic that had come so easily before, trying soft pop ("Bridge Over Troubled Water"), bluegrass ("Roll In My Sweet Baby's Arms") and pure novelty ("Monster's Holiday") in an effort to maintain the momentum, but the era had passed.

Still, he remains a popular artist on record and in concert, and has maintained high public visibility through his longtime co-hosting role in television's *Hee Haw*.

The Buck Owens sound is one which fired the imagination of many urban would-be country pickers in the mid-1960s. It is not subtle, but it is strong and filled with a sense of rollicking fun. Besides being a fine musician himself, Buck's band, the Buckaroos, were long known for their prowess, and often make his records a musical adventure. His own vocals seemed to parody himself in his later work, but his early records display singing that is both warm and sensitive.

MERLE HAGGARD

Perhaps one of the handful of authentic musical geniuses in the history of country music, Merle Haggard has achieved universal respect and admiration by remaining a maverick throughout his career. He has refused to play Nashville politics and goes his own way in the music business world.

Merle Haggard is an ex-con, loner, and blue-collar musical genius.

Born in Bakersfield in 1937, he is widely known to the public as an ex-con for the years he spent in San Quentin on an attempted burglary conviction. Following his release in 1960, he embraced the musical legacy of his father, a fiddler, and decided to become a country entertainer.

Haggard had his first hits in 1963–64. By the late 1960s he was a bona fide country star; at this point he began to assert his independence. He has an ongoing historical awareness that is matched by none of his contemporaries. Over the years, Merle has recorded tribute LPs to Jimmie Rodgers, The Carter Family, Bob Wills, and Elvis Presley. He has revived Western Swing, Cajun, classic honky-tonk, and Dixieland jazz. He has continued to speak for America's working-class, despite Nashville's uptown tendencies. He has continued to write prolifically, whereas most performers who have been around as long have long since dried up as songwriters.

His mournful vocals, arresting guitar work, admirable fiddle playing, and expert band leading have made Merle Haggard as admired a picker as he is a singer and songwriter. These qualities, combined with his charismatic, lone wolf personality have given him an aura of integrity, self-pride, and silent determination that is the envy of his peers.

SELECTED RECORDINGS

- Buck Owens
Best of Buck Owens *Capitol ST-2105*
- Buck Owens
The Best of Buck Owens & His Buckaroos Vol. 2
Capitol ST-2897
If you really want to understand the straight-ahead, no-nonsense country music of the 1960s, the *Best Of* albums of Buck Owens are the quickest way. In all, there are six of them.

Owens's lack of hits for the past half-dozen years has caused his reputation to slip badly. From 1959 to 1975, however, he was one of the real kings of the country charts. Buy these quickly, before they go out of print. Consider it a musical investment, for these tracks are all classic country; and in a very short time they'll be called "history."

The Buckaroos were one of the finest country bands in the land when these songs were recorded; and unlike many of his contemporaries, Buck *did* record with his own band, not some studio players. As for the singer/songwriter himself, he was a hill-billy delight. Owens was capable of total goofiness ("Waitin' In Your Welfare Line," "I've Got a Tiger By the Tail"), as well as country insight ("Together Again," "Under Your Spell Again"). Like his close contemporary George Jones, Buck Owens could execute rockabilly, honky-tonk, and novelty numbers with equal ease. All of those styles are audible on these superb Bakersfield style documents.

- Merle Haggard & The Strangers
Songs I'll Always Sing
Capitol SABB-11531 (two-record set)
The temptation to list dozens of Merle Haggard albums is a strong one. The man simply does not know how to record a bad record. There have been a few offhanded ones, perhaps, but even those (*Songs for the Mama That Tried, Live/Rainbow Stew,* and some other scattered examples) are consistently interesting and listenable.

The concept/tribute albums to Rodgers, Wills, Dixieland, and Carter-style gospel music are all worth owning. Several early Capitol LPs are fascinating documents of his musical progress; and *Back To the Barrooms* and *The Way I Am* on MCA are mature masterpieces. His 1980s work on CBS/Epic has been somber and introspective, but his duet albums with George Jones and Willie Nelson (also on CBS) indicate that he can still romp when the spirit moves him.

Sprinkled throughout Haggard's large LP catalog are minor masterpieces. The best first taste of his gifts, however, is on *Songs I'll Always Sing,* a double-LP compilation of his fame-making singles from 1963 to 1975. Included are his first prison-song hit, "I'm a Lonesome Fugitive"; his autobiographical hard-times songs, "Mama Tried," and "Sing Me Back Home"; and his working-class anthems, "Workin' Man Blues" and "Okie From Muskogee." From the spinetingling "Sing a Sad Song," his first single, to 1974s ineffably sad "Things Aren't Funny Anymore," this is an album to play over and over again.

OTHER BAKERSFIELD RECOMMENDED RECORDINGS:

● **Various Artists**
Country Hits of the 1960s *Capitol SM-886*
Owens and Haggard were certainly the biggest Bakersfield hitmakers, but they were by no means alone. Capitol Records' success in country in the 1960s was also due to such Bakersfield artists as Buddy Alan, Wynn Stewart, Bonnie Owens, and Susan Raye. Hit selections by all of them are collected here.

The label had a lot more going for it. Roy Clark's "The Tip of My Fingers," Glen Campbell's "By the Time I Get To Phoenix," Tex Ritter's "I Dreamed of a Hillbilly Heaven," and Wanda Jackson's "Right Or Wrong" are strong reminders of Capitol's diversity and strength. All are also included on this LP, as are Ferlin Husky, Sonny James, and Faron Young.

Chapter Thirteen
<u>Cajun Music</u>

Cajun music, redolent of steamy summer nights in the Louisiana bayous, is one of country music's most fascinating substyles, as fascinating sociologically as it is musicologically. Though strongly influenced by later folk and country music, at its heart it is the folk music of French colonists who were brutally and cruelly deported from Nova Scotia during the reign of George II—the story sentimentally told in Longfellow's "Evangeline." Many eventually settled in swampy southwest Louisiana, and due to the isolation of the area their culture, their language, and their music survived.

Th̶e̶ ̶c̶a̶l̶l̶e̶d̶ Nova Scotia Acadia, and these A̶c̶a̶d̶i̶a̶n̶s̶—̶g̶r̶a̶d̶u̶a̶l̶l̶y̶ corrupted to Cajun—brought with them a rich folk song and fiddle tradition, a tradition to which the accordion was added by German settlers passing through on their way to Texas (where there is still, by the way, a strong polka and ethnic musical tradition). This fiddle-and-accordion sound is still the basis on which the identifiable Cajun sound is based.

However, country music from the Northeast, jazz from New Orleans to the East, and Texas dance music from the West all had strong influences on Cajun music, which was recorded as early as the 1920s, once the major labels discovered there was a market for ethnic music. The sound first made a national impact with Harry Choates' "Jole Blon" in 1946—covered by many country artists, from Roy Acuff to Moon Mullican—and has continued to play a part in country music ever since, particularly in the straightforward country sounds of the Grand Ole Opry's Jimmy C. Newman, and in folk-rock's Doug Kershaw, both of whom came from deep folk roots in the area.

The insistent, heavy-bowed fiddle is one of the most identifiable sounds in country music, and Cajun music, though it occasionally tells a sad story, is primarily happy get-together dance music of Louisiana Saturday nights. Its devotees are passionate, for it is currently the closest thing to true folk music we have in this latter day and age.

HARRY CHOATES

Little is actually known about the life of the legendary Cajun fiddler Harry Choates, who grew up in Louisiana and east Texas steeped in Cajun style, and who provided the music a number of regional hits like "Poor Hobo," "Catting Around," and "Port Arthur Waltz," all Choates originals. His reworking of an old folk song, "Jole Blon," gave Cajun music its first real hit record.

A hard liver and heavy drinker, he was jailed in 1951 for wife and child desertion, and the shock of sobering up was apparently too much for his frail system (he had already developed cirrhosis of the liver in his mid-twenties) and he died within three days of his arrest at the age of 28.

JIMMY C. NEWMAN

Cajun music has found several avenues to commerciality; its avenue to pure country music was Jimmy C. Newman, born in Big Mamou, Louisiana, on August 29, 1927. After a stint on the Louisiana Hayride he joined the Opry in 1956, the veteran of one hit record: "Cry Cry Darling" (1954).

Other Newman hits followed, including "A Fallen Star" (1957), "You're Making A Fool Out Of Me" (1958), "Grin and Bear It" (1959), "Lovely Work Of Art" (1960), "Alligator Man" (1961), "Bayou Talk" (1962), "DJ For A Day" (1963), "Artificial Rose" (1965), "Back Pocket Money" (1966) and others. Though his soaring tenor is beautifully suited to straight country records, he has long been proud of his Cajun heritage, focusing on it heavily in his live shows, and having recorded a full album of Cajun folksongs early in his career.

In recent years he has gone so far as to add not only the Cajun fiddle but the accordion to his otherwise straight country band (bass, drums, steel), and this mixture gives him one of the more interesting live shows in contemporary country music, for it successfully weds some of the sound and folk roots of Cajun music with straightforward, commercially acceptable country music. One of the very few to make this combination work on an extended basis, Jimmy is still a popular and busy touring act.

DOUG KERSHAW

With such well-known songs as "Louisiana Man" and "Diggy Diggy Lo," Doug Kershaw has become the most famous Cajun musician on the contemporary scene. His jolted-by-electricity stage demeanor, outrageous personality, and bugeyed frenzy have made him an unforgettable country personality.

Kershaw was born in the Louisiana bayou country in 1937. He was raised on the folk music of that region, but by the time he was a teenager he was also playing rockabilly and straight country music with his brother Rusty. This was probably how he developed a commercial style for the music of his Cajun heritage.

Rusty and Doug Kershaw were members of The Grand Ole Opry in the late 1950s and early 1960s, but in the mid-1960s the team broke up and Doug became a solo performer. By the next decade, Doug was at least as well known and accepted among rock fans as he was to the country audience. And by the 1980s, Kershaw was a subject of some interest to the folk fans, as well.

His music is as authentic as any rural Cajun's, but he has grafted an element of show business flash and style onto the traditional music. He has also electrified his violin heavily, and dances and stomps a beat feverishly while he plays. These are doubtless the reasons that the one Cajun song most non-Cajun fans can name today is Doug Kershaw's "Louisiana Man."

SELECTED RECORDINGS

● Harry Choates
Jole Blon: The Original Cajun Fiddle of Harry Choates
D Records D-7000
In this instance, there's no selection to be made from among several LPS. This is the *only* Harry Choates album, ever; and represents virtually the whole output of this tragic Cajun genius. His brief, 1946–1951 career is summed up in the ten tracks reissued here. The classic "Jole Blon," and "Allons à Lafayette," "Louisiana," "Basile Waltz," and "Honky Tonk Boogie" illustrate why Choates is regarded as the father of modern Cajun music.

● Jimmy C. Newman
Cajun Country *Delta DLP-1144*
Although Newman's biggest hits and best known

songs were on Decca/MCA in the 1960s, in recent years he has emphasized his Cajun heritage more and more. Thus, his recent recordings are more interesting than his original Nashville Sound material to the Cajun fan. This 1981 release features him with his excellent touring band, Cajun Country. With this group he has developed a fascinating fusion between Cajun and country-rock. He spotlights the French accordion and Cajun fiddle, but underpins them with a solid, irresistable beat. Another plus is Newman's renewed emphasis on Cajun French vocals.

Like the musical hybrid Newman has created, this album is a mixture of material. Traditional numbers sit alongside newly-composed, Cajun-flavored songs; and the compatibility is impressive.

● Doug Kershaw
Cajun Way *Warner Brothers 1820*
The "Ragin' Cajun" is probably the best-known of contemporary Cajun musicians, and this album contains most of the songs that made him that. His intense, overpoweringly exuberant style and wild life at one time made him nearly as popular with the rock crowd as he was with country audiences. "Diggy Diggy Lo" and "Louisiana Man," both included here, have thus been recorded by artists from folkies to rockers to honky-tonkers.

OTHER RECOMMENDED CAJUN RECORDINGS
● Jo-El Sonnier
Cajun Life *Rounder 3049*
Like Jimmy C. Newman, Sonnier was at one time promoted as a mainstream country act on a major label (Mercury). Also like Newman, Sonnier retreated to his basic Cajun style when he began making records for smaller companies. Although he is respected in Nashville as a session musician and songwriter, *Cajun Life* was Sonnier's first real showcase as an album artist.

● Link Davis Jr.
Cajunville *DTI Records BX-2712*
This former member of Asleep At The Wheel is the son of a champion Cajun fiddler. Link features his abilities on Cajun accordion and saxophone, as well as his fiddling on this, his debut album. Although he is only half Cajun, his record is one of the most authentic-sounding of all those listed here. *Cajunville* conjures up a Louisiana house party on a Saturday night.

Chapter Fourteen

<u>Country-Rock</u>

In the late 1960s rock bands began discovering country music. This phenomenon occurred mainly on the West Coast, but country-rock also developed in Memphis and Nashville.

The reasons for the creation of the country-rock fusion style are probably two. In search of new sounds, rock guitarists became infatuated with the pedal steel guitar. And through the influence of a few key individuals, country songwriting became respected among rock fans.

One of those key individuals was Gram Parsons, a Southern-bred singer/songwriter who took his love of country songs to his long-haired musician friends in California. He joined The Byrds and transformed the group from being folk-rockers into being a country-rock band. He followed that accomplishment by forming his own band, The Flying Burrito Brothers. Groups like Poco, The Eagles, Pure Prairie League, and The Amazing Rhythm Aces followed. Others, like Commander Cody, Area Code 615, and Asleep At The Wheel refined the style with jazz and western swing elements.

None of these bands, with the exception of The Eagles, had many hit records with the country-rock sound. At the time, it was just a rock sub-style that seemed like a passing fad. Ironically, the country-rock style took root in Nashville; and it is now one of the dominant country music forms. Performers like Alabama, Charlie Daniels, Linda Ronstadt, Rosanne Cash, Juice Newton, Tanya Tucker, and Hank Williams Jr. reaped the benefits of country-rock's development by having huge country record success with variations of the style.

Like their California predecessors, these artists marry country songs to hot electric guitar licks, heavy beat, reverb-laden steel guitar sounds, and echoey vocal group harmonies.

LINDA RONSTADT

This daughter of a Tucson hardware merchant grew up with her parents' jazz collection, her neighbors' Mexican music, her friends' rock & roll records, and the country music of the Southwest. Ronstadt dropped out of college and went to Los Angeles to form The Stone Poneys, a folk-rock trio. In 1968, at the dawning of the country-rock era, she became a solo performer.

Her first three solo LPs, on Capitol Records, were country-rock milestones. Her open, wailing, teardrop-in-throat delivery was perfectly suited to country songs; and many of her Los Angeles musician contemporaries provided the mixture of intense rock playing with hot country picking.

When she moved to Asylum Records she formed a new band. This group later became The Eagles. Beginning with her second Asylum LP in 1975, Ronstadt became more eclectic, emphasizing her ability with hard rock as well as country-rock. She continued to release singles geared toward the country audience, however, until 1980 when she attempted a new wave rock album.

One of her most discussed projects was a projected trio album with Dolly Parton and Emmylou Harris. Although the planned LP never appeared, certain tracks have been on Ronstadt ("My Blue Tears") and Harris ("Light of the Stable," "Mr. Sandman") albums in the 1980s.

An album of big band standards and a Broadway operetta excursion diverted Ronstadt from country and country-rock music in the early 1980s, but she continued to feature country-rock in her concerts.

CHARLIE DANIELS

A close musical relative of country-rock is Southern rock. This style evolved in the bars of the Southeast in the 1970s and reached its apogee in the works of The Allman Brothers Band, Lynyrd Skynyrd, The Marshall Tucker Band, The Atlanta Rhythm Section, Black Oak Arkansas, and other Deep-South rock bands. The Charlie Daniels Band, alone among Southern rockers, has achieved country music stardom; and Daniels's annual Volunteer Jam which celebrates the Southern rock genre has become one of America's premier musical events.

Daniels came to Nashville to be a session musician and songwriter in the late 1960s. He had previously worked as a bluegrass fiddler and a rock & roll guitarist. Born in North Carolina in 1937, his earliest musical influences were pure country. He learned to play bar band rock later in life. The two musical strains blended to form his present style.

ALABAMA

The act that has reaped the greatest rewards of the country-rock movement has been Alabama. Essentially a Southern bar band which played the dance music of rock acts as well as the country hits of the day, Alabama adopted the close-harmony group singing and rolling rhythm of the California country-rock groups and added a Dixie flavor. With this musical mixture, the act has become the biggest-selling group in country music history.

The band is comprised of Randy Owen on rhythm guitar and lead vocals, Jeff Cook on lead guitar and keyboards and fiddle, Teddy Gentry on bass, and Mark Herndon on drums. Owen is the group's major songwriter.

Alabama was founded in the state of that name and is still headquartered in Fort Payne, Alabama; but the band made its reputation in Myrtle Beach, South Carolina, playing in bars. Persistence in mailing tapes and records of its music to various labels and producers began to pay off in the late 1970s. In 1980 Alabama began having number one records; and within two years the act won the Entertainer of the Year award from the Country Music Association, the highest accolade from the country music industry besides Hall of Fame membership.

SELECTED RECORDINGS

● Linda Ronstadt
A Retrospective
Capitol SKBB-11629
(two-record set)

The ingredients of Linda Ronstadt's country-rock came together best during the early part of her solo career. After she became a superstar in the late 1970s the country-rock style became one of many she performed.

On the Capitol Records songs recorded between 1969 and 1973, glossy Los Angeles production met and was married to Ronstadt's open-throated country voice. Always an expert at picking good songs, Ronstadt fearlessly tackled country classics like "I Fall To Pieces," "I Can't Help It If I'm Still In Love

With You," "Lovesick Blues," "Crazy Arms," and "Silver Threads and Golden Needles" during this period. Her innocence about country styles made all these familiar songs sound new again.

All of these as well as the song poet numbers like Michael Nesmith's "Different Drum," Paul Siebel's "Louise," Gary White's "Long, Long Time," and Bob Dylan's "I'll Be Your Baby Tonight" are included on this double-LP set of songs from Ronstadt's formative years. Another aspect to her art, reviving rock & roll oldies and giving them a country-type treatment, is illustrated by numbers like "It Doesn't Matter Any More," "Will You Still Love Me Tomorrow," and "When Will I Be Loved," also included.

● **The Charlie Daniels Band**
Windows *Epic AL-37694*
Million Mile Reflections, which contained the massive hit "The Devel Went Down To Georgia," is Daniels's all time biggest-selling album. But *Windows* has a stronger collection of songs and is a more coherent musical statement of what Charlie Daniels is all about.

"Still In Saigon" is pointed and opinionated, like the man who sings it. "Ragin' Cajun" and "Partyin' Gal" are quintessential Southern rock numbers. "We Had It All One Time" shows the sensitive, sentimental side of Daniels's songwriting.

Besides the famous Volunteer Jam, Charlie Daniels's major contribution to country-rock may be his ability to wed the electric fiddle to a rock beat. This and his distinctive electric guitar picking characterize all his recordings.

The ironic thing about Daniels is that even though he's Nashville, his country-rock has much more bite and edge to it than the mellow, easy-listening California rock bands who founded the style.

● **Alabama**
Feels So Right *RCA AHL-3930*
There's always at least one tender country ballad ("Feels So Right"). There's always a real barn-burning country-rock number ("Burn Georgia Burn"). There's usually an irresistible, instant classic country song ("Old Flame," "Love In The First Degree"). And there's often a musical arrangement that is nearly note-for-note in the style of the original California country-rock bands ("Hollywood," "Woman Back Home"). All Alabama LPs are the same; and as indicated by the titles listed above, *Feels So Right* is a typical. It stands out among the group's records, however, because of its consistently excellent songs.

Chapter Fifteen

The Songwriters

No matter what the stylistic genre, the foundation of all country music is the song. Discussions of honky-tonk, rockabilly, western swing, Cajun, Nashville Sound, country-rock, and other styles can illuminate country's varied musical settings; but few records in any of these genres become hits unless a strong song is the basis.

More specifically, country radio and country record buyers look for a strong lyric. Traditionally, a country fan could say, "That song is about me," or "I know just what he's singing about," about a favorite record. The emphasis on lyric content was such that non-country fans frequently criticized country music of the 1950s and 1960s as "all sounding the same." Accustomed to pop music variety, uninitiated country music listeners have difficulty directing their aural attention to words, rather than musical arrangements. This has become less true in recent years, but despite new studio sounds on country discs, the meaningful song remains the heart.

Country music honors its most gifted songwriters as no other form of music does. Nashville has a songwriters' Hall of Fame, a televised award show devoted to songwriters, five major banquet/award ceremonies for songwriters annually, and innumerable workshops, clinics, and round table discussions among its tunesmiths. More than a record capital, more than a studio center, more than a live music scene, Nashville is first and foremost a song city. Songs and music publishing are the soul of Music City's music business.

Several of country music's major stars have acquired their reputations at least as much because of their songwriting gifts as by their performance styles. Surrounded by the trite and the banal, these artists have fashioned moments of poetry and laser-sharp insight from the simple ingredients of a country tune.

WILLIE NELSON

He sold his songwriting rights to "Family Bible" and watched helplessly as it became a huge hit in 1960. "Night Life," "Funny How Time Slips Away," "Crazy," and "Hello Walls" all enriched his songwriting reputation and his pocketbook as artists like Ray Price, Patsy Cline, and Faron Young recorded them; but he got little recognition. Willie Nelson always thought he was a good singer, himself, however. Nashville being the songwriters' town that it is, Nelson was able to get a recording contract; but he spent 15 long years trying vainly for a hit record.

Willie Nelson's unique bluesy style has won him a vast audience.

Part of the problem was that his eccentric, off-the-beat, jazz-influenced phrasing was at cross purposes with the easy-listening, string-arranged Nashville Sound style. Another problem was Nelson's live performance style. Never a master of show business flash, Willie was an essentially shy man who preferred to have his songs speak simply and eloquently for him.

He did develop a following in the beer joints of Texas, however. And at last, fed up with Nashville's overproduced commerciality, he moved there to make records according to his own vision of the Willie Nelson sound, dominated by his gutstring guitar runs and solid rhythm section.

From 1975 on, the records he created achieved astounding popularity. Nelson ascended far beyond being a country star, becoming a multimedia celebrity and building a following so broad that every LP he released was a million-seller. Now recording a combination of his own songs and tried-and-true pop music standards, Nelson is the Sinatra of this generation.

ROGER MILLER

Like Willie Nelson, Roger Miller was a songwriting pioneer in Nashville. They rose through the ranks in the early 1960s together, succeeding despite their sometimes quirky, sometimes rebellious natures.

Both were born in Fort Worth, Willie in 1933 and Roger in 1936. Miller came to Nashville first, attempting to break into the music business there in the mid-1950s. He worked as a bellboy while trying to establish himself as a songwriter. By the late 1950s he had written songs for George Jones, Andy Williams, Ray Price, Ernest Tubb, and others. These early compositions, like "Invitation To the Blues," "In the Summertime," "Lock, Stock, and Teardrops," and "When Two Worlds Collide" demonstrated some interesting rhythm and word patterns, but in the main were like other country hits of the day.

After moderate success as a recording artist on RCA, he changed labels to Smash Records. At this time his songwriting style changed dramatically as well. He began to allow his wacky sense of humor and speedy word salads to creep into the songs he wrote for himself. Immediately, he became a sensation.

"Dang Me," "Chug-a-Lug," "Do Wacka Do," "England Swings," "King of the Road," "Kansas City Star," and a string of top-sellers in the mid-1960s earned him multiple accolades, including an astounding 11 Grammy Awards. Later songs such as "Husbands and Wives" and "Walkin' In the Sunshine" indicated that he had not lost his gift for serious songwriting, but his record popularity faded in the 1970s.

In 1982, he and old cohort Willie Nelson recorded a duet LP for Columbia called, appropriately, *Old Friends.*

KRIS KRISTOFFERSON

Perhaps no Nashville performer better illustrates the deep respect that the city has for songwriters than Kris

Kristofferson. Although he did not write "typical" country songs, he was embraced by country singers. Although he cannot sing well in any conventional sense, he was promoted into being a successful recording artist.

Kristofferson is frequently touted as the most "literary" of country music's songwriters. College-educated and well brought up, he nevertheless struggled on the streets of Music Row with the rest of his songwriting generation in the late 1960s.

While he was working as a janitor at Columbia Studios, his songs slowly gained him a reputation as a talent to watch. Roger Miller was one of the first to record a Kristofferson song, "Me and Bobby McGee." Johnny Cash did Kris's "Sunday Morning Coming Down." Then Sammi Smith made his "Help Me Make It Through the Night" into an international hit.

Despite his vocal limitations, Kristofferson made a successful transition to being a recording artist. His own version of "Why Me" won him a gold record. Others continued to take his tunes up the charts, too. Brenda Lee's "Nobody Wins," Ray Price's "For the Good Times," and Janis Joplin's "Me and Bobby McGee" are examples.

Kristofferson is widely cited as the Music City songwriter who broke down lyric barriers. His words are direct, frank, sometimes sexual, and always honest; and he seldom relies on the word plays and double meanings often used by traditional country writers.

TOM T. HALL

There is a certain literary quality about the songs of Tom T. Hall, too. He has titled some of his albums *I Witness Life, The Storyteller, The Rhymer & Other Five-and-Dimers,* and *In Search of a Song,* which gives some notion of the kind of narrative songs he creates.

Born in Olive Hill, Kentucky in 1936, Hall has an authentic mountain background. From his preacher father he inherited a sharp eye for the foibles and follies of his fellow man. When he began to write songs, he frequently drew on his observations of life, of the colorful characters he'd met, or of situations he'd experienced. His ballads earned him a reputation as a tale-spinner and he confirmed this by publishing several books, including a novel, after he became a star.

Hall has often expressed his love for bluegrass music, and his records have frequently been graced by expert acoustic instrumental passages. He also has a predilection for concept albums.

DOLLY PARTON

A true child of Appalachia, Dolly Parton was born in East Tennessee in 1946. Performing on local radio and at small churches while still a child, she made her first record by the time she was a teenager.

Dolly came to Nashville the day after she graduated from high school. When Bill Phillips made a hit of her "Put It Off Until Tomorrow" in 1966 she was on her way as a songwriter.

As a recording artist, she began as a country/pop singer on Monument Records; but after she joined the hard country Porter Wagoner show as female vocalist

Dolly Parton is one of Nashville's most successful crossover acts.

and duet partner, she became more country-oriented on RCA. In the mid-1970s her sensitive lyrics and fragile-rose vocal delivery made her a solo star.

In the late 1970s she made her move toward pop music stardom with a series of Los Angeles-influenced albums. In the early 1980s she made the transition to Hollywood movie celebrity status, and concurrently began adapting her music to films.

As a songwriter, Dolly Parton generally uses lilting, folk-influenced melodies. As a child, her favorite tunes were rockabilly numbers, however, and this also sometimes shines through her compositions. Her lyrics are generally extremely insightful, her themes ranging from children's feelings to women's issues, from pastoral odes to biting social commentary.

LORETTA LYNN

Like Parton, Loretta Lynn is her own best interpreter. Although few of her compositions have been recorded by other artists, several of Loretta's songs have become country classics simply through her versions.

Lynn began her professional career after spending a dozen years as a wife and mother. Married at age 13, she was 25 when she arrived in Nashville to become a singing star because of the urging and promotion of her husband. By the mid-1970s she was the most honored and awarded woman in the history of country music.

She achieved multimedia celebrity status when her autobiography, *Coal Miner's Daughter,* became a best-selling book and an Oscar-winning film in the late 1970s. Instead of cashing in on this success, though, Loretta just kept on doing what she had always done, touring the country tirelessly, wailing her honky-tonk heartache laments, and behaving with the humility, humanity, and humor that have endeared her to millions of country music fans.

Her genius as a lyricist is her piercing honesty. Loretta has never been one to beat around the bush about anything; and she has tackled subjects in song that few of her female contemporaries dared to. Although her song output in the 1980s has diminished, she has already left two decades worth of timeless tunes.

SELECTED RECORDINGS

- Willie Nelson

Yesterday's Wine *RCA ANL-1-1102*

His breakthrough record was *Red Headed Stranger,* but it contains relatively few Willie Nelson compositions. His world-famous *Stardust* and *Somewhere Over the Rainbow* are collections of pop music standards done Willie-style. Even *Willie Nelson's Greatest Hits* includes only "Good Hearted Woman," "Angel Flying Too Close To the Ground," and "On the Road Again" as Nelson originals.

All of those are beautiful records. They're all on Columbia and are made just the way Willie wanted them. It was not always so at his previous record label, RCA. Nevertheless, he made a few landmark recordings while he was with that company. One was his *Panther Hall Live* LP, and another was this record, *Yesterday's Wine.*

Few of the songs on *Yesterday's Wine* are well-known Nelson compositions, but all are minor masterpieces. The album is a quasi-religious "concept" record, recorded in 1971. They're thoughtful, wistful songs, the kind that even other songwriters would sit up and take notice of. Producer Felton Jarvis wisely let the songs do the work, and Nelson and his band, for once, were allowed to carry the record without "assistance" from string sections and background vocalists. Willie is at his reedy, nasal best as a singer; and as a songwriter he was never better than on this album.

● Roger Miller
Golden Hits *Smash SRS-67073*
In just two years, from 1964 to 1966, Roger Miller released "King of the Road," "Dang Me," "Engine, Engine #9," "England Swings," "Chug-a-Lug," "Do-Wacka-Do," and "Kansas City Star." All were big pop music hits as well as country music smashes. And all were textbook examples of clever country songwriting.

"King of the Road" illustrates country music's concern for the commonplace, the ordinary details of life, as it spells out the existence of a hobo. "Dang Me," "Chug-a-Lug," and "Do-Wacka-Do" are good illustrations of country music's fascination with word-play and humorous rhymes. "Engine, Engine #9" takes the oft-repeated country theme of trains and goodbyes and gives it a different twist. "Kansas City Star" and "You Can't Rollerskate In a Buffalo Herd" (also included on this LP collection) are part of what can only be described as country music's "goofball" tradition. A version of one of Miller's early songs, "In the Summertime," is on this album as well. It demonstrates Miller's gifts as a composer of mainstream Nashville material as well as of brilliantly eccentric tunes.

● Kris Kristofferson
Songs of Kristofferson *Monument PW2784-38392-1*
Kristofferson's rasping shred of a voice is all that is needed to put these songs across—they're that powerful. "For the Good Times" is so poetically sad it can reduce you to tears. "Lovin' Her Was Easier" has lines that can match those of the great bards. "Help Me Make It Through the Night" and "Sunday Mornin' Comin' Down" are so graphic and real you can almost touch them. Kristofferson is a tunesmith who could have become a star only in Nashville, for where else could he have gotten a hearing based purely on the strength of his words and images?

● Tom T. Hall
Greatest Hits *Mercury SR 61369*
Virtually any Tom T. Hall album made before 1975 is a priceless collection of country songwriting gems.

His ability to paint portraits in song of living, breathing people was matchless during that era. Hall is a reporter, a witness. He seldom draws morals or conclusions. He merely illuminates the lives of ordinary people in three-minute melodies. "I Washed My Face In the Morning Dew" asked questions about life. "The Ballad of Forty Dollars" depicted a country funeral. "The Year That Clayton Delaney Died" ennobled a small-time musician. "The Homecoming" was a masterpiece of self-revelation as an entertainer returns to his humble roots and realizes he's been transformed. These and more vignettes crowd this collection of perfect country lyrics.

- Dolly Parton
Coat of Many Colors *RCA LSP-4603*
- Dolly Parton
My Tennessee Mountain Home *RCA APL 1-0033*

To really understand Parton's genius as a country songwriter, skip most of her recent output and seek out these two LPs from the early 1970s. The title tune of *Coat of Many Colors* tells the tale of a rag coat her mother made for her one winter. It also includes a dark song of madness called "If I Lose My Mind," a beautifully sad little masterpiece called "My Blue Tears," and a weird spiritualist song called "The Mystery of the Mystery."

My Tennessee Mountain Home is a concept LP about Parton's past. It begins with a vision of Nashville ("Down On Music Row"), then delves deeply into hard times and poverty ("Daddy's Working Boots," "In the Good Old Days") as well as precious memories of her girlhood ("Dr. Robert F. Thomas," "I Remember," "My Tennessee Mountain Home").

Some of these tunes were collected on the first volume of her *Greatest Hits* albums (there have been three). Of Parton's newer albums, *Heartbreak Express, 9 To 5,* and *New Harvest, First Gathering* showcase her songwriting best.

- Loretta Lynn
Greatest Hits *MCA-1*
- Loretta Lynn
Greatest Hits Vol. II *MCA-420*

Lynn has never been the most gifted or innovative of melodists. But she more than makes up for this with her artful, to-the-point lyrics. This most country of country songwriters has kept alive the topical song tradition.

On the first volume of her greatest hits, for instance, she tackles the Vietnam War ("Dear Uncle Sam"), woman/woman violence ("You Ain't Woman

Enough"), alcohol ("Don't Come Home a Drinkin' "), and turnabout-is-fair-play female sass ("Happy Birthday").

Greatest Hits Vol. II includes her famous autobiographical songs "Coal Miner's Daughter" and "You're Lookin' at Country," as well as her delightfully feminist allusion to her Indian ancestry "Your Squaw Is On the Warpath."

Wit and warmth characterize Loretta and her songwriting. They frequently overshadow her impressive vocal abilities. When she's thought of at all as a singer, it's usually as a female honky-tonker. Some of the non-originals on the second album, such as "Love Is the Foundation" and "One's On the Way," illustrate that she has a much wider emotional range and can handle a variety of tunes expertly.

Chapter Sixteen

The Outlaws

Austin, Texas has a much livelier live music scene than Nashville, Tennessee; and Texas audiences are far more enthusiastic and demonstrative than their Volunteer State counterparts. Austin is also less bound by musical categories. Many favorite musicians there have country roots, but mix their music with dashes of rhythm & blues, rock & roll, Mexican, or other genres. They are a freewheeling, unclassifiable lot.

In the 1970s, several mainstream Nashville performers who were dissatisfied with the sameness of music in the country capital began to look favorably upon the Austin scene. Willie Nelson moved there and built a recording studio which attracted likeminded country musicians. Rather than paying attention to country formulas, these artists made music Austin-style, without regard for musical labels.

The media began referring to the Nashville rebels as "Outlaws" because they were making different-sounding country discs. Willie and Waylon Jennings were the first to wear the new label; but Johnny Paycheck, David Allan Coe, Tompall Glaser, and others soon joined them. "Outlaw" was never a distinct musical style, merely a handy term to give to longhaired country musicians who broke away from the Nashville Sound.

WAYLON JENNINGS

Waylon Jennings is a West Texas native (b. 1937) who spent his early music career dividing his time between being a disc jockey and singing in night clubs. At age 21 he moved to Lubbock, Texas and joined Buddy

Waylon Jennings broke the Nashville mold with his
charismatic personality and music.

Holly's band The Crickets. When Holly died, he returned to radio work.

Much has been made of this rock & roll influence on
his style, but Jennings's personal brand of country
music didn't really develop until he moved to Phoenix
and began performing full-time. His crack band The
Waylors was formed at this time and the distinctive
Jennings sound evolved. To Waylon's fullbodied, ro-
bust singing voice a heavy rock beat, characterized by
a steady "walking" bass guitar line, was added.
Rounding out the sound was penetrating steel guitar.

Spotted in Phoenix by Bobby Bare, Jennings was
brought to Nashville by Chet Atkins in 1966. He
scored minor hits almost immediately, but only
achieved superstar status when he began taking
charge of his own recordings in the mid-1970s.

Although quite gentle in person, Jennings's erratic
personality, avoidance of the press, and refusal to play
Music Row politics have given him a tough-guy public
image. His rock-oriented kind of country music also
frightens conservative Nashville; and he keeps his
distance from the music business scene of his city.

HANK WILLIAMS JR.

Hank Williams died when his son was only three-and-
a-half years old, but Hank Williams Jr. grew up in his
shadow nonetheless. Before he was even a teenager his
mother Audrey had him on stage doing imitations of
his father and performing his father's songs.

Hank Jr.'s musical influences were much broader, though. He was particularly impressed with the blues and learned to play piano and guitar in that style as well as country. He began writing his own songs in the mid-1960s and gradually these began to replace Hank Sr.'s in his repertoire.

Not until Audrey died in 1975 did he emerge as an individualist. Following his recuperation from a near fatal mountain accident that same year, Hank Williams Jr. released a series of superb Southern rock records that owed a great deal more to the sound of The Allman Brothers than to Hank Williams.

By the dawn of the 1980s, Hank's redneck rock had made him one of the most popular performers in contemporary country music. In 1982 he placed eight of his albums on the popularity charts simultaneously—a previously unheard-of feat.

He has developed into a marvelously expressive singer and an impressive multi-instrumentalist. Still a young man, he shows no sign of letting up as an opinionated, topical country songwriter, and promises to be one of the principal creative forces in country music of the coming decades.

SELECTED RECORDINGS

- Waylon Jennings
Greatest Hits *RCA AHL-3378*
This album spans Jennings's recording career from his seminal albums of 1973–1975 (*Honky Tonk Heroes, This Time,* and *Dreaming My Dreams,* all highly recommended) to 1979. His stirring, pounding country-rock anthems "I've Always Been Crazy," "Good Hearted Woman," and "Are You Sure Hank Done It This Way" are the album's centerpieces. But Jennings's equal brilliance as a vocal balladeer is spotlighted on tracks like "Amanda" and "Luckenbach, Texas."

Waylon's skill as an electric lead guitarist is much in evidence on these hits; and his well-known duet with Willie Nelson, "Mamas Don't Let Your Babies Grow Up To Be Cowboys," is another highlight.

- Hank Williams Jr.
Greatest Hits *Elektra 60193*
Like Waylon, Hank Jr. is capable of great tenderness as well as rollicking rock. "Old Habits," included here, is ample proof of that.

But Hank's snarling, howling rockers are what have endeared him to country music's youth market. "Dixie On My Mind," "A Country Boy Can Survive," and "The American Dream" certainly fill the bill on that account; and they're also outstanding examples of his prickly, pointed politics.

He has never completely abandoned the legacy of his father. "Family Tradition," was a landmark Hank Jr. performance since it drew explicit parallels with Hank Williams Sr.'s legendary excesses and those of Hank Jr. and his outlaw Southern rock crowd. In addition, he turns his father's classic "Kaw-Liga" into a churning rocker with a killer of a backbeat.

OTHER RECOMMENDED "OUTLAW" RECORDINGS:

● David Allan Coe
Greatest Hits *Columbia KC-35627*
Principally known as the songwriter of Tanya Tucker's "Would You Lay With Me" and Johnny Paycheck's "Take This Job and Shove It," Coe is also a remarkably effective country singer. He has never had a major hit, but this collection demonstrates that it isn't for lack of trying. Coe's nasty biker image is a little too much, even for fans of Outlaw Country; but he has made consistently fine records. He eschews the rock influences of most of the other "outlaws," and instead concentrates on making excellent, straight-ahead, stone country singles.

● Johnny Paycheck
Biggest Hits *Epic FE-38322*
Paycheck was an established mainstream country singer when the so-called outlaw movement occurred. He had been a member of George Jones's band and had several solo hits prior to the mid-1970s. He embraced the outlaw image eagerly, however, even changing his middle name to "Austin" to increase his credibility with long-haired young country fans. He backed this up with a series of aggressive singles that dealt with prison ("11 Months & 29 Days"), violence ("Colorado Cool-Aid"), drink ("Drinkin' and Drivin' "), and rebellion ("Take This Job and Shove It"). All are included on this compilation.

Chapter Seventeen

Pop-Country

Contemporary country music is many things. The honky-tonk tradition survives in the work of John Anderson, George Jones, John Conlee, Gene Watson, and George Strait. Ricky Skaggs and his followers have injected new vitality into the bluegrass tradition. Acts like Riders In the Sky and Rex Allen Jr. ensure that cowboy music stays alive. Country-rock is flourishing, with artists like Rosanne Cash, Charlie Daniels, and Waylon Jennings enjoying tremendous sales with different varieties of the genre. Carl Perkins, Sleepy LaBeef, and Jerry Lee Lewis continue to pound out rockabilly; and they're being joined by a host of young rockabilly revivalists. On small country labels like Rounder, Flying Fish, and Sugar Hill you'll find dozens of bands reviving the sounds of western swing, classic Cajun, old-time string band music, and every other historical country style.

What dominates on country radio these days, though, is a modern mixture of country and pop music. This is not just a continuation of the Nashville Sound style. Rather, it is country-trained musicians trying their hands at pop music. Their overwhelming success in doing this has led to a blurring of musical categories in recent years; and now many say that "country" is more a record company marketing term than a description of a type of music. Pop-country artists take their musical inspiration from all over the pop music spectrum. They share, however, country music's veneration of the well-crafted song; for all of these artists continue to draw material from America's capital of song, Nashville.

GLEN CAMPBELL

The father of pop-country is unquestionably Glen Campbell, for he was the first post-Nashville Sound artist to take country songs to the top of the pop charts. Born in 1936, Glen was raised in hard-luck circumstances the equal of any country star's.

He began his career as an instrumentalist, succeeding first as a country/bluegrass picker and L.A. studio guitarist. Possessed of one of the most beautiful, heart-filled tenors in popular music, he soared to the top of the charts in the 1960s with both West Coast singer/songwriter material and straight country tunes. Although based in acoustic music, the arrangements for these were lush with strings and echo.

Campbell parlayed disc success into television celebrity, movie star, and gossip magazine status. But he also continued to grow as a musician, developing into a fine composer and bagpipe player.

CHARLIE RICH

Charlie Rich has never really fit comfortably into country music, despite decades in the business. He began his recording career on Sun Records as a rockabilly act, and then attempted soul music. With

Charlie Rich, the Silver Fox, plays and sings blues and jazz as well as country.

the aid of Nashville pop-oriented production and some can't-miss romantic ballads, Rich became a pop-country crooner in the mid-1970s. When left to his own devices, however, he prefers to play Oscar Peterson-type piano jazz.

Rich's hallmarks are his thin, whiskey-burned, pleading voice and his dextrous piano playing. He is known as The Silver Fox for his cool demeanor and elegant shock of white hair.

ANNE MURRAY

This ex-gym teacher from Nova Scotia was initially surprised by her acceptance on country radio and among country music fans: She had never considered herself a "country" artist until her records became country hits. She has taken to the medium well, however, and habitually chooses Nashville songs and producers for her records.

Murray is an alto with meticulous diction and perfect pitch. A cool, aloof blonde, she nonetheless is capable of investing songs with great feeling. She achieves this by combining her flawless vocal technique with sparkling musical arrangements that spotlight her chesty lows and throaty highs at dramatic lyric moments.

She was born in 1946 and has spent her entire life in Canada, despite U.S. record stardom. She states repeatedly that Toronto home life with husband and children is more important than her musical career.

KENNY ROGERS

In the career of Kenneth Ray Rogers is the apotheosis of pop-country stardom. Middle-aged Kenny (b. 1938) worked his way from doing teenage song material to Houston lounge jazz to folk-revival New Christy Minstrel membership to pop First Edition success before he got around to country music in the late 1970s. When he finally did, he became the biggest selling recording artist on earth.

He's from the wrong side of the tracks in Houston, but now he occupies the rarified celebrity atmosphere of a Sinatra or a Presley. He got there by judicious song selection, specializing in lush, florid love songs and in country narratives. Kenny's soft rasping singing voice gives these conviction.

BARBARA MANDRELL

This petite blonde was trained to be an entertainer from the time she was a child. Mandrell initially attracted attention as an adept instrumentalist. She demonstrated steel guitars at trade shows.

Although born in Houston, she was long associated with the Southern California scene, where she made her first record and radio appearances. Following her move to Nashville in the late 1960s, Barbara tried to gain prominence by doing country-flavored interpretations of soul songs on Columbia Records. When this failed, she garnered her first big hits with more conventional country material. After she moved to MCA Records, however, she dusted off soul oldies once again; and she has since established her musical fame as a slightly hoarse interpreter of bluesy numbers and jaunty pop-flavored tunes. Mandrell plays several instruments skillfully, but not on her albums.

THE OAK RIDGE BOYS

Begun as the Oak Ridge Quartet in postwar Tennessee, the group was a longtime leader in gospel music. In the 1960s the name was changed to The Oak Ridge Boys; and numerous personnel shifts occurred. The lineup stabilized in 1973; and this Oaks version—Bill Golden, Duane Allen, Richard Sterban, Joe Bonsall—won every gospel music award possible.

In 1976-77, the quartet made the transition to country music. Then in 1981 the single "Elvira" made the Oaks pop music stars as well.

Through it all, the sound has remained that of an exhortative gospel quartet. The four-part harmonies with individuals stepping out for solos have been continuous; but the musical backing has become more and more pop/rock oriented in recent years.

EDDIE RABBITT

Raised in New Jersey, Eddie Rabbitt (his real name) was taught guitar by his scoutmaster. After a brief stint as a New York pop recording artist on Date Records, Rabbitt decided to concentrate on his songwriting and moved to Nashville.

His first successes in Music City came as the composer of Ronnie Milsap's "Pure Love" and Elvis Presley's "Kentucky Rain," both number one hits. After these, he formed a songwriting partnership with Even Stevens; and the two began experimenting in the studio with producer/songwriter David Malloy. The results won Rabbitt an Elektra Records contract; and country and pop stardom ensued.

His sound is characterized by jangling rhythm guitar, multitracked vocal harmonies, and rock rhythms. Rabbitt's voice is rather light and airy, but he enhances it with expert production and an emphasis on the rockabilly end of the country music spectrum.

CRYSTAL GAYLE

Although she is the baby sister of the stone-country Loretta Lynn, Crystal Gayle grew up in the family's second home in Indiana, not in Kentucky Appalachia. Consequently, she was more influenced by pop warblers like Leslie Gore and Brenda Lee than she was by pure country singers.

It was to eliminate confusion with Brenda Lee that she changed her name from Brenda Gail Webb when she signed with her big sister's record label. She tried to make it there as a country singer; but after she switched labels and developed her own style, she became a star. That style is derived from cabaret singing and pop stylings, and is characterized by odd pronunciation and a certain "hurt" in her throat.

RONNIE MILSAP

Born blind, Milsap was raised in North Carolina with a variety of musical influences. A child prodigy, he could play violin by age seven, piano by age eight, guitar by age twelve, and several woodwind instruments by his late teens. Milsap has classical music training, but his first love was rock & roll. With three other blind students he formed his first band, The Apparitions.

After achieving some success as a studio musician in Atlanta, he moved to Memphis to become a popular nightclub performer. His first impact as a recording artist was as a rock and white soul singer.

He made the transition to country music on RCA in the mid-1970s, and initially performed strictly in that idiom. By the dawn of the 1980s, however, Ronnie's pop/rock roots reasserted themselves and he began having hits with ballads, rockers, and soul songs.

DON WILLIAMS

A terse, soft-spoken Texan, Williams maintains the image of a decent American family man religiously. His tender ballads and calm, thoughtful delivery reinforce this; and the gentle, loping tempos of his tunes suggest a serious, sane, sensible personality.

Williams, like several other current country stars, is a product of the 1960s folk revival. His band, The Pozo Seco Singers, was one of many folk trios of that era.

He achieved country stardom with a crisp, simple sound dominated by guitar, mandolin, and dobro underscored by a rolling bass line and a soft-rock drum beat. In England, this approach has made him as appealing to pop fans as country devotees.

SELECTED RECORDINGS
- Glen Campbell

The Best of Glen Campbell *Capitol ST-11577*

This collection includes the three songs that cata-
pulted Glen Campbell to fame, "Gentle On My
Mind," "Wichita Lineman," and "By the Time I Get
To Phoenix." It stops briefly at "Galveston," the
finest song of his middle period; then leaps ahead to
his late 1970s classics "Rhinestone Cowboy" and
"Country Boy (You Got Your Feet In L.A.)."

Three different production teams are represented, but all of them maintained the Campbell
mode of pushing the vocal up to the front in the
sound mix, virtually to the exclusion of distinct
background instruments. Instead of hot licks, what
you remember instrumentally about Glen Campbell
records is the soaring, high violin section serving as
a backdrop.

- Charlie Rich

Behind Closed Doors *Epic KE 32247*

This album contains all you need to know about
Charlie Rich as a pop-country hitmaker, for it con-
tains the giants ("Behind Closed Doors," "The Most
Beautiful Girl") that put him at the top of his field.
For a more in-depth look at this eclectic stylist, seek
out his Sun recordings (still available on various
Greatest Hits sets) or his Memphis discs on Hi
Records.

Rich doesn't overpower a song. He breathes and
sighs lyrics softly, as though they were a natural part
of his life. Therein lies his greatness.

- Anne Murray

Let's Keep It That Way *Capitol R-123663*

All Anne Murray albums have several things in
common. They are always superb collections of
songs, frequently from a fairly wide variety of musical genres. They are always brilliantly produced,
with meticulous sound and just enough "edge" to
keep them interesting. And they are always showcases for one of the prettiest voices in pop-country.

This LP is an Annie archetype in that it contains a
bit of country ("Tennessee Waltz"), some gorgeous
contemporary melodies ("You Needed Me," "You're
a Part of Me"), a dash of nostalgia ("Walk Right
Back"), and a hint of soul music ("I Still Wish the
Very Best For You").

- Kenny Rogers

Greatest Hits *Liberty L00-1072*

Can there be a person alive today who has not
hummed along with "Lucille" and "The Gambler"?

These, along with "Coward of the County," are Rogers's most country recordings of recent years. Two songs from his days with The First Edition *should* have been country hits, but weren't because Kenny was a pop act back then. New recordings of these, "Reuben James" and "Ruby, Don't Take Your Love To Town," remind us of Rogers's past.

Lest we forget his status as a crooner of pop romantic ballads, Rogers's "She Believes In Me," "You Decorated My Life," "Lady," and "Love the World Away" are presented in all their lush glory.

● Barbara Mandrell
The Best of Barbara Mandrell *Columbia 34876*
Barbara's recent work on MCA Records has strayed further and further from straight country music. And her status as a television celebrity has emphasized her nightclub chanteuse aspects.

This album of her 1971–1975 work for Columbia, however, indicates that those qualities have been present in her style virtually from the day she arrived in Nashville. "This Time I Almost Made It" and "Scarlet Water" are ballad showcases. "Treat Him Right," "Show Me," and "Do Right Woman, Do Right Man" are remakes of soul songs in the Mandrell style. She has done these continually in her career. There is a *Best Of* album available on MCA that contains her more recent hits. Although there are two different producers on these two *Best Of* packages, it is interesting to note that Mandrell's essential style has remained constant.

● The Oak Ridge Boys
Greatest Hits *MCA 5150*
This is the Oaks just after their graduation from gospel music into country and just prior to their elevation to pop star status. The group's first country hit, "Y'All Come Back Saloon," is one highlight of the set. Its good-time country style is echoed in "Come On In" and "Trying To Love Two Women." "You're the One" also has this rousing, revival, hand-clapping quality. "Leaving Louisiana In the Broad Daylight" is a step toward pop record-making.

● Eddie Rabbitt
The Best of Eddie Rabbitt *Elektra 6E-235*
Rabbitt's recent work might cause some befuddlement about how he came to be identified as a country act. This collection of his first hits demonstrates how this came to be.

"Drinkin' My Baby (Off My Mind)" "Rocky Mountain Music," and "Two Dollars In the Jukebox," all from 1976 (the first year he hit the country top ten), could have been hits for any hard country artist. "Hearts On Fire," "You Don't Love Me Anymore," and "We Can't Go On Living Like This," from the 1977–78 period, are the kind of melodic, soaring tunes that seem to do well on both country and pop charts. But by the time of 1979's "Every Which Way But Loose," there's more on the pop side of things than on the country. This set cuts off at that point. The next *Best Of* will pick up with "Drivin' My Life Away," pop-rockabilly that pleased both camps.

● Crystal Gayle
Classic Crystal *Liberty LN-10150*
The cabaretlike, almost vaudevillian "Don't It Make My Brown Eyes Blue" made Crystal a pop star. But the most appealing tracks on this set are the singer's lazy, loping country-tinged hits "Somebody Loves You," "You Never Miss a Real Good Thing," "I'll Get Over You," "Wrong Road Again," and "I'll Do It All Over Again." The pop-rocker "Why Have You Left the One You Left Me For" closes the album, hinting at more rock-type material to come.

● Ronnie Milsap
Greatest Hits *RCA AAL-1-3772*
Like so many country stars and Southern-bred musicians, Milsap is a master of many styles. He can be a soulful shouter ("Let My Love Be Your Pillow"), a mainstream country stylist ("A Legend In My Time") or a pop lounge balladeer ("It Was Almost Like a Song") with equal ease. More than anything else this collection illustrates that Milsap is a bundle of musical contrasts. He can be light and trivial one moment with something like "Back On My Mind Again," then turn around and drench the listener with the devastating emotion of "Please Don't Tell Me How the Story Ends."

● Don Williams
The Best of Don Williams Volume II *MCA 3096*
There are two Greatest Hits collections available on Don Williams. The first, titled simply *Greatest Hits,* spans 1972–1976, the years of "Amanda," "I Recall a Gypsy Woman," and "The Shelter of Your Eyes."

This one contains some of his more recent hits. Most Don Williams records sound alike, but for some of the numbers on this set the tempo is a bit brighter ("Tulsa Time," "Say It Again") or the lyrics are especially poignant ("She Never Knew Me," "Some Broken Hearts Never Mend"). Thus, it has the edge over the first hit-loaded set. Williams' gentle baritone and tasteful instrumental mixture makes listening to his records a continually reassuring, comforting experience.

RECOMMENDED READING

Chances are, once you've been hooked on country music from listening to it, you'll want to learn more about it and its history. Luckily, there are several excellent books on the market to lead you deeper and deeper into the country music world. They fall into four basic categories. Books from journalists and observers of the Nashville scene are perhaps the best places to start your reading, for they convey the flavor of this fascinating culture best. Because the past is more important to country music than to any other American popular song tradition, the history books are essential reading. The various encyclopedias are volumes you will turn to again and again for information on country stars. Country musicians have fascinating stories to tell about their lives, so the biographies and autobiographies listed here are both revealing and educational.

JOURNALISTS' BOOKS AND GENERAL WORKS

Guralnick, Peter. *Lost Highway: Journeys & Arrivals of American Musicians.* Boston: David Godine, 1979. 362 p.

Hurst, Jack. *Grand Ole Opry.* New York: Abrams, 1975. 403 p.

HISTORIES OF COUNTRY MUSIC

Carr, Patrick and the editors of **Country Music** magazine. *The Illustrated History of Country Music.* Garden City: Doubleday, 1979. 359 p.

Malone, Bill C. *Country Music, U.S.A.: A Fifty Year History.* Austin: University of Texas, 1968. 422 p.

COUNTRY MUSIC ENCYCLOPEDIAS

Dellar, Fred & Roy Thompson with Douglas B. Green. *The Illustrated Encyclopedia of Country Music.* New York: Harmony/Salamander, 1977. 256 p.

Stambler, Irwin. and Grelun Landon. *Encyclopedia of Folk, Country, and Western Music.* New York: St. Martin's Press, 1983. 396 p.

BIOGRAPHIES AND AUTOBIOGRAPHIES

CASH, JOHNNY: Christopher S. Wren. *Winners Got Scars Too: The Life of Johnny Cash.* New York: Dial Press, 1971. 252 p.

LEWIS, JERRY LEE: Nick Tosches. *Hellfire.* New York: Dell, 1982.

LYNN, LORETTA: Loretta Lynn with George Vecsey. *Loretta Lynn: Coal Miner's Daughter.* New York: Warner, 1976. 256 p.

NELSON, WILLIE: Lana Nelson Fowler. *Willie Nelson Family Album.* Amarillo: H.M. Poirot and Co., 1980.

PARTON, DOLLY: Alanna Nash. *Dolly.* Los Angeles: Reed Books, 1978. 275 p.

PRESLEY, ELVIS: Jerry Hopkins. *Elvis.* New York: Simon and Schuster, 1971. 446 p.

RODGERS, JIMMIE: Nolan Porterfield. *Jimmie Rodgers: The Life and Times of America's Blue Yodeler.* Urbana: University of Illinois, 1979. 460 p.

WILLIAMS, HANK: Roger Williams. *Sing a Sad Song: The Life of Hank Williams.* New York: Ballantine, 1973. 275 p.

WILLIAMS, HANK JR.: Hank Williams Jr. with Michael Bane. *Living Proof.* New York: Putnam, 1979. 222 p.

WILLS, BOB: Charles R. Townsend. *San Antonio Rose: The Life and Music of Bob Wills.* Urbana: University of Illinois, 1976. 395 p.

WYNETTE, TAMMY: Tammy Wynette with Joan Dew. *Stand By Your Man.* New York: Simon and Schuster, 1979. 349 p.

INDEX